CELEBRATING HER

CELEBRATING HER

Feminist Ritualizing Comes of Age

Wendy Hunter Roberts

The Pilgrim Press
Cleveland, Ohio

The Pilgrim Press, Cleveland, Ohio 44115

Published 1998. All rights reserved

Printed in the United States of America on acid-free paper

03   02   01   00   99   98   5   4   3   2   1

Library of Congress Cataloging-in-Publication Data

Roberts, Wendy Hunter, 1948–
    Celebrating her : feminist ritualizing comes of age / Wendy Hunter Roberts.
      p.   cm.
    Includes bibliographical references and index.
    ISBN 0-8298-1258-X (pbk. : alk. paper)
    1. Goddess religion—Rituals.   2. Feminism—Religious aspects.
  3. Feminist spirituality. 4. Witchcraft. I. Title.
  BL473.5.R63   1998
  291.3'8'082—DC21

98-14596
CIP
Rev.

CONTENTS

FOREWORD

Marjorie Procter-Smith

We know ourselves to be made from this earth. We know this earth is made from our bodies. For we see ourselves. And we are nature. We are nature seeing nature. We are nature with a concept of nature. Nature weeping. Nature speaking of nature to nature.

—*Susan Griffin,* Woman and Nature

As persons living at the end of the twentieth century, in a highly technological age, we sometimes like to imagine that we have somehow sprung ourselves free of our tether to the earth and its natural cycles of growth and death and decay. As persons living at the end of the twentieth century in a highly complex and diverse world, we sometimes tell ourselves that our society had risen above the gender struggles and quests for identity that motivated earlier movements for the rights of women. And at the same time, we experience a hollowness at the core, perhaps; a longing for mystery and drama, for meaning and relationship. Women, even those who retain a sense of connection with traditional religions, sometimes experience a lack within the ritual practices of those traditions, a silence, an absence, about the deepest truths of themselves and their lives as women. And it is this sense of something missing that leads people, both women and men, all over North America and beyond to gatherings of the sort that this book describes and critiques: nature-based rituals. We have forgotten, but are starting to rediscover, that, in the powerful words of Susan Griffin, "we are nature seeing nature."

In this book, Wendy Hunter Roberts places before the reader two tasks: first, to examine and consider the value of recovering a sense of being part of nature and of experiencing that connection in ritual terms; and second, to evaluate the extent to which nature-based and Goddess-centered rituals are or can be feminist rituals— that is, rituals that offer women access to ritual power, energy, and meaning. She then invites the reader to accompany her in the planning, execution, and subsequent assessment of eight different nature-based rituals. We look over her shoulder as she evaluates each context and community as well as the place the ritual will occupy in the natural cycles of the earth in the Northern Hemisphere. We participate vicariously in a rich variety of ritual events, from the modest winter solstice observance of a small Unitarian Universalist church to the ambitious Festival of First Fruits public concert in Golden Gate Park. And we share in her evaluation of these diverse rituals, as she unflinchingly critiques rituals she has helped plan and lead, naming the parts that were ritually ineffective as well as those that she (and the participants) saw as effective. In particular, she raises feminist questions about these rituals, deftly articulating the social and political implications of ritual and symbol.

Who should read this book? Anyone who has ever wondered about what nature-based religion and ritual is about. They will learn that nature-based rituals can be created that speak to persons of varieties of religious background; that our nature as creatures binds us together beyond the commitments to creed or tradition that often divide us; that we are "nature with a concept of nature." They will encounter the rich symbolism available in the cycles of light and darkness, of birth, death, and decay, that have given shape and meaning to life on earth since the beginning of all things. And those whose religious identity is grounded in biblical religion will find that the basic symbols of those traditions draw on these same cycles and natural symbols: light and darkness, life and death. Hunter Roberts's Goddess-oriented, nature-based rituals offer tantalizing hints of what contemporary biblical religions might look like if they reclaimed the power of these primordial symbols with the same energy with which Hunter Roberts claims them.

Who should read this book? Anyone who seeks to understand what is so attractive about nature-based rituals to persons who find traditional religious ritual boring or irrelevant. They will see just where the missing pieces of the religious puzzle lie: in claiming and naming the experiences of women as religious experience; in connecting the life cycles of human beings with the cycles of earth; in offering drama and play and deep challenge within a religious context. They will see what happens when ritual is designed to take respectful account of the members of the community who will be participating in it, when the process of planning is collaborative, when the planners are self-critical and reflective about every ritual event.

Who should read this book? Anyone who is interested in the workings of ritual and symbol in our contemporary technological age. The academic study of ritual has its roots in anthropological study, and anthropological study, in turn, has its roots in the field study of pretechnological, even preindustrial, societies. For a long time, we denizens of the post-industrial, technological, post-Enlightenment West have imagined that we are much too sophisticated and advanced to need ritual. We have told ourselves that ritual is the activity of prescientific, "primitive" people, an activity we have surely outgrown. But more recent scholarship has called these assumptions into question, pointing out the inevitability of ritual activity among all animals, both human and nonhuman. Indeed, some contemporary writers have gone beyond arguments of inevitability to arguments of necessity. The title of Tom Driver's book sums it up: *The Magic of Ritual: Our Need for Liberating Rites That Transform Our Lives and Our Communities.* The rituals created and evaluated by Hunter Roberts in this book attempt to transform lives and communities, and provide ample evidence as well of the resurgence of interest in ritual, particularly religious ritual.

Who should read this book? Anyone who wants a feminist analysis of contemporary nature-based ritual. Feminist rituals have a long history of expressing a relationship between women and nature. Within the Western androcentric intellectual tradition, at least, women have long been identified with nature, to the detriment of both. Both women and nature, in a male-centered universe, have been understood to be unruly, anarchic, and dangerous unless carefully controlled—by men, of course. As feminist rituals and feminist spirituality began to develop a distinctive voice in the West, this woman–nature connection became part of what was to be reclaimed, not as a danger but as a strength. Thus feminist rituals often employ natural objects and outdoor settings, and make use of metaphors and symbols drawn from natural cycles. Such rituals and spiritualities, however, for all their strengths, often tend to fall into a romanticized notion of both nature and women, accepting the androcentric notion that women are "closer to nature" than men, and that nature itself is simple, accessible, and always agreeable. To her credit, Hunter Roberts avoids this trap, exemplifying a commendably complex understanding of both the blessings and the risks involved in claiming the deep human connection with the cycles of nature. In the design, in the leading, in the evaluation of each ritual, the complex relationship between humans and the rest of nature is evoked, recalled, observed, experienced. Hunter Roberts speaks often, and eloquently, about her knowledge "in the bones" of the deep meaning of the natural cycles her rituals evoke. But it is clear that this knowledge includes the knowledge that we are nature, but nature is not us. It is something larger and less tamable than anything human-made. The symbols generated by nature have power because they present the mystery of natural cycles of life and death, cycles beyond our control and even ultimately beyond our intellectual understanding.

Contemporary revivals of Goddess worship have likewise sometimes fallen prey to the patriarchal tendency to romanticize (the reverse of demonizing) the Goddess image, to locate in a female deity all the patriarchal virtues assigned to women. Hunter Roberts is rightly critical of these approaches, insisting instead on a feminist approach to Goddess worship that is clear about the power inherent in symbol-making. And as is perfectly clear in her rituals and her self-critique, the process of symbol-making often requires symbol-breaking as well: the breaking of destructive personal symbols, or shattering of limiting social symbols, or disrupting of comfortable but shallow religious symbols. Like an eggshell, they break only to give life to something new.

Where will the rituals of the sort described in this book go? What will become of the practices created and sustained (or not) by the various communities for whom they have been created? It is tempting to prophesy, or perhaps to dream. But such activities go well beyond the demands of a foreword. Suffice it to say that the future of these rituals and others like them, and the future of the collaborative and self-critical process presented here, is now in the hands of the readers of this book. This is no collection of recipes for persons who want to start their own ritual communities. It provides no simple, "fill-in-the-blank" formula for creating ritual. Instead, it offers something more challenging, and perhaps more dangerous: a hint, an open door, an invitation to readers to claim the transformative power of ritual and symbol, to understand that this power is irrevocably collaborative, and that its entire purpose is to bring about justice and peace and dignity for women and for all of life.

PREFACE

This is a book about transformation and empowerment. It investigates the forms and symbol structures of nature-based, Goddess-centered ritual. A dozen or so years ago it occurred to me that myth, ritual, and symbol could—and did—transform the world. The Goddess was not new to me, even then. I had long seen God as a woman, having read Eugene O'Neill's *Strange Interlude* in my teens, and having been a feminist thinker and activist since 1969. I had been influenced by the radical paradigmatic shift suggested by early writings in the field of feminist spirituality. Indeed, it informed my counseling practice and my social change work. But I did not practice or ritualize in any tradition. When asked, I said that my work for social and personal transformation was my spiritual practice, and this was true.

I had made occasional forays into Wiccan covens, but found myself frankly repelled by the arcane customs and personal brouhahas I encountered there. I had also made forays into progressive Jewish and Christian services, but found myself at odds with the God whose promotional literature credited "him" with the destruction of the temples and peoples of the Goddess. Even though I found much to resonate with in the texts and practices of Buddhism, it did not call to me as a religion. And Unitarian Universalism, while in line with many of my values, did not ritually or spiritually satisfy. In the end, like many of my progressive and feminist contemporaries, I decided ritual and religion were a little hokey. Then influences converged to cause a complete turn in the direction of my life.

It happened in 1985. Feminists were losing ground. Geraldine Ferraro had been soundly put in her place, abortion rights were being challenged, Phyllis Schlafly was flying high, and Star Wars was going forward under the most popular president ever elected. The rise of fundamentalism was in its first blush, influencing military policy toward Armageddon with the deployment of first-strike nuclear weapons in Europe. Attendance was falling off in mainstream, liberal churches. Televangelism was peaking. The so-called Moral Majority was a force to be reckoned with, while feminist and progressive politics seemed to have no place to stand. Like it or not, the religious right was onto something.

Most of my friends and colleagues scoffed that fundamentalist religion offered ignorant people easy answers. But I saw a kind of moral authority in the language of symbols and archetypes that the religious right wielded in their worship services and campaigns. I attended some of those services, and real power was present in the music and precognitive manner of their delivery system. It was ritual, complete with repetition, invocation, swelling music, and rising energy. It put people in touch with something beyond our power to name it. Then opportunistic right-wingers used the name of Jesus for ends that, as far as I could tell, had little to do with the teachings of the Gospels. This ritualizing was being used to undermine the most important gains of the feminist and environmental movements.

It was while contemplating all this and wondering how to regain the moral high ground for a message of harmony and liberation that I was invited to attend my first nature-based ritual. It was a simple garden-planting ritual celebrating the spring equinox at a primitive retreat center in Northern California. The genuine spiritual power of the invocations to nature's elements—earth, air, water, and fire—and the authenticity and beauty with which people sang and celebrated the Goddess, not as a person, but as the generative life force in all growing things, resonated through my body, causing tears to roll down my cheeks. For the first time I felt seen and honored as a woman in a religious ceremony. I was at home in a symbol system.

In this and subsequent experiences, including an all-night workshop and prayer circle climaxing in a walk across hot coals that did not burn, I experienced firsthand the power of ritual, rebinding me to my life at a time when I had come unbound. The symbols entered my soul through song and imagery in a way that they never could have through mere concept. Here was a worldview honoring the feminine that could speak powerfully to all people, and a symbol system rooted in nature that we all could recognize through our own bodies. Here was really old-time religion as practiced in the West long before Christian missionaries baptized it into Christianity as All Saints' Day, Christmas, and Easter. Here was a way of communicating an ethos that could empower women and inspire humans to live in harmony with, rather than dominate, the earth.

I began to pray for direction, and I received it in no uncertain terms. "Take the jewel to the Lady" was my instruction, given through guided imagery, which I translated to mean "Return the earth to the Goddess." I had some learning to do if this was my task. I entered seminary. In the years since 1986, I have studied, explored, and experimented with inclusive and empowering ritual forms through which to celebrate and reflect on the human relationship to the generative life force, which I call the Goddess, of which we are all a part. I explored images and containers that were empowering to woman and to nature, and which rebound us to our home, the earth. I committed to finding and creating a broad range of images of the female divine that would reflect us back to ourselves as powerful and sacred, in order to place into the culture an icon of the female essential, the primary generative force in the universe, no longer the "other."[1]

My explorations have been for the most part rooted in the nature-based, Goddess-centered symbol system often referred to as Neopagan, used by most North American practitioners of nature-centered spirituality. Because it is rooted in nature and because it worships both a female and a male image of deity, this symbol system has within it forms and symbols that reflect a more holistic and inclusive view of the sacred. I find these forms and symbols to be a useful template for any spiritual and celebratory practice that wishes to reach beyond the limiting patriarchal, hierarchical, anthropocentric model that has dominated worship for centuries. I believe that these symbols transcend their European Wiccan origins.

We know them in our bones, for they are nature based, and so are we. They go back much further than the Middle Ages in Europe, and exist similarly among all indigenous, earth-worshiping peoples of both hemispheres.

Even so, I have not left behind my Jewish and Christian sensibilities entirely, but have sought to make connections whenever possible—as my story of seeking a recipe for the cakes for the Queen of Heaven (chapter 1) indicates. I have wanted to develop ritual expressions that are accessible to all sorts of people, women and men, young people, people who know themselves by a variety of faith traditions. Much as I love and am personally at home in a circle around the fire at night, I realize that most people are not going to join such circles, or wear robes and capes, or participate in anything that they believe smacks of witchcraft.

So I have set myself to the task of translating these ancient symbols into modern American, urban culture without losing their power or numinosity. I have pushed the ritual forms this way and pulled them that way in my attempts to evolve a deeply rooted and accessible, feminist form of celebrating that reconnects us with the essence of life. I wished to call on, without imitating, the roots of Wiccan practices, just as I wished to honor and call on, without appropriating, non-European indigenous traditions. This book is a chronicle as well as a critique and analysis of some of my ritual explorations over the past dozen years.

This book examines and critiques contemporary nature-centered spirituality and Goddess rituals from a feminist perspective. I have set myself two main goals in this book: first, to describe one year-long cycle of nature rituals informed by feminism for those who are only now becoming aware of this nature spirituality (which preexisted and has been long buried inside Christian and other traditions), and, second, to assess the ways in which these rituals and spirituality can inform other traditions and practices in the cause of women's empowerment.

Investigating the power dynamics and symbols of Goddess-centered, nature-based ritual through comparing and contrasting, I ask throughout: "Does this symbol/form empower women?" and "Is this ritual effective/Does it 'work'?" I have critiqued the rituals from the point of view of aesthetics, believing that bad theater is seldom good ritual.[2] I have attempted to uncover the underlying assumptions about the nature of ultimate reality, subjecting every ritual action to the question, from a feminist perspective, of what is being done and why. I have looked from the perspective of whether the rite affirmed nature- and life-supporting values, asking: Does it increase the odds on the Life of Life?[3] Through this inquiry it is my hope that readers will develop both constructive and critical faculties for working with ritual, liturgy, and symbols in a context of feminist empowerment. In so doing, women claim religious authority to use the power of rite and symbol to empower themselves and their sisters.

ACKNOWLEDGMENTS

In this process of remembering and inventing feminist ritual several persons have been particularly helpful. Among the many who deserve thanks are Nancy Ellis, my agent and champion; Joan Levinson, Susan Alexjander, and Susan Maloney for their reading and thoughtful comments; Marjorie Procter-Smith for her encouragement and her wonderful foreword; Orion Stormcrow, Oberon and Morning Glory Zell, and the staff at Green Egg for their ready generosity in sharing information and resources; Jess Shupe for helping to track down authors of obscure chants; Rebecca Salome for wise advice and encouragement; Anodea Judith for refuge and good counsel on both writing and ritualizing; Kay Jorgensen for support in countless ways; Clare Fischer and Joanna Macy for their unflagging belief in my work and their years of mentoring; the faculty and students at Immaculate Heart College Center for giving me the opportunity to develop many of my ideas; Ye Ye Ife, Wanda Lee, and Diane Darling for their partnership in creating some of the rites described herein; Rick Hamouris, my ritual priest and partner for the entire period covered in this book, who supported my work with his creative genius and his rhythmic power; The Pilgrim Press for its willingness to stretch beyond the map and see the territory we share; Timothy Staveteig, my editor, for his wise, brave, thoughtful, patient, and respectful editing and advocacy, and for his willingness to work with a symbol system that must have seemed foreign at times; and finally to my beloved teacher, Rev. Dr. Wayne Rood, whose understanding of the depth and power of worship has inspired and informed every piece of ritual or theater I have done since I had the good fortune to be his student. To him this book is respectfully dedicated.

Part

1

Feminist Ritualizing
Comes of Age

SHE WHO RULES THE SYMBOLS ROCKS THE WORLD

As I was going through some old files one day, a paper caught my eye, a program from a conference long since forgotten. It was an early, maybe the earliest, New York City conference on women's spirituality, in the mid-1970s. I thought, "Have we really been doing this for more than twenty years? Well, then, the movement must be grown up. We have reached the age of our majority—haven't we?"

✳ THE WOMEN'S SPIRITUAL MOVEMENT COMES OF AGE ✳

Imagine! It was 1971 when Z. Budapest formed the original Susan B. Anthony Wiccan coven, inviting women of the Los Angeles Women's Center to join her in a feminist religion. In 1973 Mary Daly challenged the fundamental assumptions of conventional religion and theology with *Beyond God the Father*. Many women first encountered in 1976 an ancient image of the divine that was radically different from today's patriarchal god, with Monica Sjöö's *Cosmic Mother* and Merlin Stone's *When God Was a Woman*. In 1977 a courageous Episcopal bishop in New York ordained the first dozen women as priests in an unauthorized ceremony that put the patriarchal church into a tizzy from which it is still reeling. That same year Carol Christ keynoted "The Great Goddess Re-Emerging Conference" in Santa Cruz, California, with her now classic essay "Why Women Need the Goddess." Starhawk's 1979 book, *The Spiral Dance,* shared with the world, for the first time, rituals, exercises, meditations, and philosophy of neo-Wicca for a nature-based, female-honoring, sex-positive religion. So much has happened in these years.[1]

The Movement's Accomplishments

What has been the upshot since 1971 of these years of feminist metaphysics and religious critique? What has been accomplished in these years of women ritualizing? Looking around for signs, I do not need to look far. My own professional existence is evidence of a change in the weather for feminist spirituality. I was accepted into and graduated from an accredited seminary as an open devotee of the Goddess, and now that is a common occurrence. Conferences of the American Academy of Religion now regularly include panels and papers on feminist theology, feminist ritualizing, the Goddess, and nature spirituality themes. The California Institute for Integral Studies in San Francisco has a graduate program in women's spirituality, and Immaculate Heart College Center in Los Angeles has a master's program in feminist spirituality. These are important milestones in the growth and recognition of a reemergent women's tradition.

Scanning my bookshelves, I see writings on feminist liturgy and ritual by Mary Collins, Rosemary Radford Ruether, Marjorie Procter-Smith, Janet Walton, and Charlotte Caron—women who have carved out and defined the territory for feminist liturgy and ritual in the academy. I see popular books by Luisa Teish, Z. Budapest, Starhawk, and others teaching how to ritualize in various Goddess-centered forms. I can find more books and journals devoted to the Goddess movement and tradition in women's spirituality bookstores and in women's spirituality sections in other bookstores. These did not exist twenty years ago.

The nature spirituality movement has also grown. Twenty-five years ago there were a few small, scraggly bands of hippies celebrating sun and moon up in the hills. Now there are national Neopagan churches, journals with circulations of up to 20,000, chat groups on the Internet, large conferences and festivals, and stores selling Goddess figurines, books, and ritual items for the practice of Goddess- and nature-based magic.

Of all the signs on the horizon, perhaps the most interesting are the countless homegrown women's spirituality groups that have sprung up all across the nation and beyond. (I am told such groups even exist in Brazil and Ireland.) Women everywhere are exploring spirituality and ritual rooted in a female image of the divine. From Woman Church to Wicca, these groups have spread quietly underground like mycelium, developing their own strands of female-centered worship and ritual to empower women in their lives.[2]

In the past twenty-five years women have reclaimed a history many thousands of years old, in which women were honored as spiritual leaders and embodiments of the divine. A Goddess figurine from Willendorf, Germany, marks a sacred tradition going back twenty-eight thousand years. Frescoes of masked priestesses in what is now eastern Turkey tell us that women performed the rites of birth and death for their community nine thousand years ago. Women now can call on the tradition of women's ritual and religious leadership in the priestesses of Sumer and Crete, and the medicine women and healers of Africa and the Americas. Feminists have found Christian foremothers among the Flemish Beguines of the fourteenth century and among courageous women heretics and mystics in all eras who dared to assert their right to define their own relationship to the sacred in the face of male institutional authority and sometimes certain death. Women have claimed and mourned their heritage as wise women and healers in the countless European women burned as witches between the fourteenth and eighteenth centuries.[3]

In these years of circling and sharing, many women have recovered their sacred selves and a sacred sisterhood, mirrored in the face of the Goddess. We grew strong and found our own voice. We created our own forms, naming ourselves and asserting our own identity. We affirmed ourselves and each other. We claimed religious autonomy apart from male institutional approval. We grew up.

What, then, are the rights and duties of adulthood? First comes independence, then comes interdependence. The women's spirituality movement has achieved liturgical independence in these years of ritualizing. Now it is time to move into the public realm of interdependence with what we have learned. We have something to contribute to the world that may be of vital importance to future generations.

The Movement's Future

When I look around the women's spirituality movement I see mostly women of my own age. Where are our daughters? For that matter, where are our sons? Do we not have something to offer them? If feminists were to take on religious leadership, putting the feminist critique into practice proactively in the larger world of ritual and symbol making, future generations of young women would have the opportunity to know their own divinity in the form of the divinely empowered female. Future generations of men would view women's bodies with respect, and honor the wisdom of their minds, as a result of education through and into a feminist worldview and symbol system.

Imagine what life would be like, what women's senses of their own bodies would be, if they had been raised not on the story of Eve's sin but on the story of the Great Cosmic Mother giving birth to the sun, the moon, and the stars. Imagine telling daughters and granddaughters stories about Mother Earth's labor to give birth to all the plants and animals. Imagine knowing oneself to be substance of her substance, blood of her blood, feeling one's own femaleness to be sacred every day of one's life. Imagine the world if this were the language, framing, and symbol system used and understood by society in general. Would this not radically shift current values, institutions, and priorities? Would human beings not have a different view of female sexuality? Would it not alter the human relationship to nature? If the minister called God "she" on Sunday morning, would that alone not give women more confidence in themselves?

Now let us look hard at the daily world in which most Americans live their lives. Consider most suburban churches, a chamber of commerce meeting, or a Toastmasters' breakfast. Have a conversation at the office water cooler and see how much knowledge of feminist spirituality or the Goddess is shared. Notice, even, how much inclusive language is used in prayer and God-talk. Most people still talk in terms of "God, he." Most of the world is still unaware of and unaffected by what has been loosely grouped and defined as the women's spirituality movement of the past twenty or so years. Feminist theology and spirituality are not yet impacting the larger world at a level that will make much difference for future generations. Practitioners are still talking to mostly to themselves.

Conversations within a community of shared values are good and useful, but they are not enough. To make an impact on that world, feminists will need to enter a domain from which they have been excluded. They will need to become citizens and assume leadership for that domain—the world of symbols, ideas, and archetypes (called religion), made flesh through their enactment in sacred ceremony (called ritual). It is not an accident that the patriarchal church holds so tightly the ritual reins. "The patriarchal church controls the line that cannot be crossed by women. Feminist ritual confronts the tradition and taps into spiritual imagination."[4] Citizenship in this world would give women full power to name and wield the archetypes that shape us and our lives.

We now constitute a mature movement. With maturity one develops the independent skills, judgment, and emotional balance to care for oneself and the next generation. Through concern for the young, true maturity moves one into the realm of interdependence, calling adults to become public citizens, leading and shaping the human future. Citizenship requires women to involve themselves in the common good, as they realize that the good of all those they care for can ultimately be secured only from within the public realm.

As a movement, feminist ritualists and thealogians ("thealogian," "thealogy," and similar forms relate to the feminine Goddess, in contrast with the masculine form "theo-") are now old enough to vote for their vision of the future. It is time for feminists to claim the rights and responsibilities of religious citizenship—ritual and religious authority in the public realm. It is up to powerful women with feminist vision and values to transform the face of religion.[5]

* THE NEED FOR FEMINIST RITUAL EFFICACY *

Reaching maturity calls for some changes in the way women are doing things. One of the distinguishing characteristics of feminist ritual and liturgy, according to Mary Collins, is that it is not text bound.[6] Indeed, one common lament by scholars working in the fields of feminist liturgy and ritual across a variety of faiths, cultures, and symbol systems is that few texts are available. Even though some such texts have been destroyed, women in general simply do not seem to record what they do in sacred ceremony. Rather, they allow it to emerge in process. Then, after the rite is performed, they move on without stopping for formal analysis, critique, or documentation. Reasons for this dearth of textual records include the following:

* Feminists in general reject fixed or rigid forms, as not meeting our needs or empowering us.
* Women view ritual as organic, emerging from the people and situation at hand, and thus having little or no value outside its indigenous context.
* Because they internalize their subordinate status, women tend not to value their work sufficiently to see its worth for others.
* Women's ritual traditions have been passed down orally because in many cultures women have had little access to literacy or the tools of analysis until recently.
* Female-centered rites have often been performed in secret, against the sanctions of the dominant culture, making documentation dangerous.

If women are to become more widely recognized as ritual and religious leaders, if feminist ritualizing is to be extended into religious institutions and the larger culture, if existing religious rites are to better reflect a feminist and nature-based perspective, then analysis and reflection will need to be undertaken. Theological suppositions and effects will need to be articulated; the effectiveness of ritualizing events will need to be critiqued: Does this adequately implement a feminist vision? Does it empower and liberate women to define and shape our world?

Women will have to defy history and historically bound inclinations to take our places within the growing discourse on liturgy and ritual. We have long been outsiders in the domains that define reality. Marginality has its comforts, enabling us to kibitz from the sidelines while "doing our own thing" in relative comfort. For the most part the women's spirituality and nature spirituality movements have been spontaneous, organic, and largely without reflection on the nature or long-term usefulness of what it is we are doing.

Much of what has been written recently in the field of women's, Neopagan, or nature-centered ritual has been of the cookbook variety, how-to books without much reflective consciousness. As in the early stages of many things, women's ritual has flourished in the absence of self-consciousness and outside stares. This has been both safe and exciting!

But now, as the movement for women's spiritual self-empowerment reaches the age of its majority, it is time to reflect on what we have been doing, to examine our rites for efficacy, for their underlying assumptions about the nature of ultimate reality, and for their feminism. It is time that we became clear and intentional about our purposes and values. It is time to claim our place in the mainstream culture and marketplace of ideas. This will require a willingness to engage critically with our own ideas and forms. We will first need to identify the value in ritualizing. Then we will need to define what we are doing and why we are doing it, in dialogue with other ritual and symbol systems.

✳ CONSTRUCTING A RECIPE—AND A TRADITION ✳

The story behind Cakes for the Queen of Heaven (chapter 6) provides but one example of being intentional and in dialogue with other ritual and symbol systems. Diane Darling, my friend and co-priestess, and I had been searching for a central symbol to use in a public rite we were scheduled to perform at Immaculate Heart College Center for the spring public event of 1996. We had named it "Return to the Mother," in honor of Persephone's return to her mother, Demeter, [7] because it fell on the eve of the vernal equinox (in the spring when the sun crosses the equator and when day and night are the same length; around March 21), when Persephone's return was traditionally celebrated.

We intended to use the date to provide a ritual opportunity for women to return to a female image of the sacred in the form of the Mother Goddess. When Diane told me she had learned at a workshop that the Hebrew Scriptures provided a recipe for cakes offered by the Hebrew women to their Goddess, Asherah, [8] I was too excited to be cautious. A communion sharing these ancient Semitic cakes would be the ideal symbol for women of mixed traditions returning to their Mother. By reclaiming a symbol out of the Hebrew tradition and combining it with a story out of Pagan Greek tradition, we could invite all the women present to affirm their own mothers and the Mother of us all. It seemed the perfect unifying symbol to bring together biblical and Goddess traditions in an overarching feminist theme empowering to all women.

The symbolic value of the cakes comes from a passage in Jeremiah. The story takes place during the Babylonian exile, after the destruction of Jerusalem and Judah, when some of the people of Judah have migrated to Egypt. Their God, Jeremiah says, has been offended by the people's sacrificial offerings to other gods, and for this reason he has brought down great destruction upon them. The women dwelling in exile answer Jeremiah's accusations and threats, saying,

> "As for the word that you have spoken to us . . . we are not going to listen to you. Instead, we will do everything that we have vowed, make offerings to the Queen of Heaven and pour out libations to Her, just as we and our ancestors, our kings and our officials, used to do in the towns of Judah and in the streets of Jerusalem. We used to have plenty of food, and prospered, and saw no misfortune. But from the time we stopped making offerings to the Queen of Heaven and pouring out libations to Her, we have lacked everything and have perished by the sword and by famine." And the women said, . . . "Was it without our husbands' approval that we made cakes for Her bearing Her image and poured out libations to Her?" (Jeremiah 44: 16–19, capitalizations mine)

This passage makes clear that honoring the Goddess was as surely a part of the Judeo-Christian tradition as of the Celtic one. Her worship was especially vital to the Hebrew women prior to the Babylonian exile. She has been exiled from us by centuries of patriarchal monotheism and speaks between the lines in a *subjugated voice* that is finally being raised up. (The current, widespread movement among Catholic laity urging Pope John Paul II to declare as dogma that Mary is co-redeemer with Jesus is, I believe, another attempt to retrieve the Queen of Heaven, albeit in a slightly watered-down form.) By reclaiming this long lost symbol of female divinity and our historical connection with the women of Judah who honored her, Jewish, Christian, and Goddess-worshiping women together could reclaim and honor their Mother. [9]

The idea of serving the cakes sent chills up my spine. I supposed that the moon-shaped cakes had not been baked and offered by women in a long time, maybe thousands of years. Reclaiming and redeeming such a powerful symbol went right to the heart of my commitment to develop symbols and ritual that empower women. But I was concerned lest such a communion to the Goddess be considered blasphemous or idolatrous by the Christian women who I expected would comprise the majority of guests at this public gathering. I wanted then—as I do in this book—to empower all women to take this powerful symbol of female divinity into their traditions and practice, using it to transform the thousands of years of dominant patriarchal symbols. If a ritual act offends more than it empowers, it is not appropriate or useful.

I remark on this because for feminist ritual to be truly such it must empower the relationships between and among women.[10] I was the guest of a Christian-based institution, teaching and performing ritual from my Goddess-centered tradition. It was no small risk that the chair of the feminist spirituality master's program had taken in inviting me to teach and perform a large public ritual there, and this had not passed unnoticed. It would not serve the cause of feminism to have her job or department threatened by thoughtless actions on my part. The symbol of the cakes must be understood to unite rather than divide the vast range of women who would be attending, or it would not empower anyone.

I called Immaculate Heart College Center and explained what I wanted to do. Could the director and the institution stand behind such an audacious act? Sister Susan did not hesitate. She sent the story to the school's public relations director, who interviewed me and promptly sent a release to the *Los Angeles Times*. The next thing I knew, the story that we were going to serve cakes for the Queen of Heaven made from an ancient biblical recipe had been printed in the *Times*'s weekend edition. This had better be good!

Our planning began in earnest. A week or two before the equinox, I began my search for the recipe in question. I knew it was not in the Jeremiah passage because that passage was already familiar to me. Although I had never encountered such a recipe elsewhere, I had little doubt it was tucked in some other mention of pre-monotheistic sacrificial rites or the battles over Asherah in the temples. I called my friend. Who was her source of this information? She was not certain, but she referred me to the woman who had led a particular workshop at the conference. I located the workshop leader. To my dismay, she claimed never to have said such a thing. Perhaps one of the workshop attendees?

I began to fear that I was in trouble. With a week to go and no recipe, the *Los Angeles Times* article had prompted a flurry of phone calls to the college, making the attendance projections rise to three times their usual size. If I did not produce what I had promised, the scholarly credibility of the sponsoring institution could be compromised, not to mention my own credibility and that of the tradition I represent. Poring over biblical books at the Graduate Theological Library in Berkeley, I became increasingy desperate for a biblical reference or a scrap—anything—that could offer a lead to this mysterious recipe.

After several hours of research, I realized my worst fears were true. Not even allusions to such a recipe were to be found in any Bible. Either Diane had misunderstood what someone had said, or the story was apocryphal altogether. In either case, I was in trouble. I had to figure out some honorable resolution.

Slowly I began to approach the concordances again, no longer hoping for a complete recipe, but for clues. What would the cakes have been made of? I knew from my research on Demeter, the Greek grain goddess, that barley was said to be the grain sacred to her, and that it was the first grain to be cultivated and stored in the ancient Near East. It was also the first grain each year to ripen and be harvested. I figured that the cakes might have been made of barley. Because barley was the first grain cultivated, and the Goddess was, in most traditions, the first deity worshiped, it stood to reason that cakes to the Canaanite goddess would have been made of barley, too, just as the ones offered to Demeter were.

Sure enough, there were references in the concordance to barley cakes being baked and offered in high places. My excitement rose as I found references to honey cakes, raisin cakes, and fig cakes being burned on high altars by the Canaanites to their gods. I found references to women kneading and baking special loaves as offerings. I found books and dissertations on Canaanite customs of worship and sacrifice.

Slowly, painstakingly, being careful to reference and cross-reference, I began to piece together a recipe of how the cakes might have been made: barley (sprouted or ground into flour? I tried both) sweetened with honey, raisins, and figs, then leavened and seasoned with coriander, their most treasured spice. What for leavening? It was clearly a kneaded cake, so I found wild yeast from an ancient Egyptian strain to leaven the sweet bread in the certain absence of baking powder. What for liquid? Goat milk or water. And for fat, local safflower oil had been available in the land of Canaan. The most confounding question was: What had they used as a binder? There were no chickens being herded through the desert, so eggs were not an option. Neither did the ancient Semites have tofu as a substitute. Finally I settled on goat curd. I was taking liberties, but there had been references to goat curd in other parts of the Hebrew Scriptures, even if not in relation to bread or cakes.

I bought the ingredients in a natural-food store and took them home to experiment. I had not planned to put this kind of time into this part of the project, nor have I ever been known for my talents as a baker. Still, it seemed the only thing to do. If the central symbol of a ritual is hastily concocted, without integrity toward what it represents, the whole ritual will lack the power of integrity and intention. I tried this way and that, with mixed, and sometimes inedible, results. Diane tried other combinations in her kitchen 150 miles away, regularly calling to compare notes.

Step by step, piece by piece, we assembled our ingredients like archaeologists carefully reassembling a pot long broken, trying to make each piece fit the next with as much integrity and authenticity as possible, but in the end having to resort to filling in with our imaginations. I kneaded and punched, adjusting flavorings as I went, making sample after sample, until at last I rolled out and cut with a glass (in place of a clay pot or shard) one hundred fifty small crescent-moon-shaped cakes to honor the Queen of Heaven. When finally they were arranged on a platter, tasting strange yet good, I wept as though some long-forgotten part of my memory and my self had returned to me.

It was then I realized that the reclaiming of this symbol and reconstruction of the recipe to bake the sacred cakes was itself a metaphor for reowning our religious heritage as women, emblematic of the whole feminist project of women's history. We were recreating a lost past. Of course the recipe was not whole, any more than our history as women can be found whole. That was lost or destroyed long ago. Of course women cannot simply look up our heritage in patriarchal texts and pass it on to our daughters. It will continue to require painstaking work, piece by piece, shard by shard, to reclaim what was lost. Sometimes, like the archaeologist, we shall have to guess at what might have been, and fill in with the clay of imagination. I recalled the passage I had read so long ago in Monique Wittig's *Les Guerillères:* "There was a time when you were not a slave, remember that. . . . You say there are no words to describe this time, you say it does not exist. But remember. Make an effort to remember. Or, failing that, invent."[11]

* THE EIGHT RITUALS *

The rituals described in this book are examples of such a combination of remembering and inventing. Chapter 2 provides a guide to symbolic reality and the basic functions of ritual—elements that combine in a particular process or event to build a transformed or affirmed world, through the manipulation of symbolic language in a contained space. We explore at some length the relationship of feminism to symbol-making, and why feminists must engage in symbol-making activities if we are to transform our world. We also discuss what makes a ritual feminist, and the differences between " feminist" and "feminine" spiritualities.

Chapters 3 through 10 consist of descriptions and analyses of eight rituals I have facilitated or participated in over the past dozen years. To give the reader a sense of the variation that is possible in leadership and liturgical style, I have deliberately chosen to present the broadest possible range of ritual styles in the rites included. One is a ritual in which I was a participant rather than a primary creator. The other rituals were created and facilitated by me with the help of various co-leaders. The styles and ritual voices vary widely, running the gamut from small, private holy day, to public rock 'n' roll concert; hence the voices of the descriptions may also vary. This book is about ritualizing, which occurs in groups of all shapes and sizes. What the rituals have in common is their order of service and their implicit or explicit symbol system. Each ritual described includes the eight elements found in most ritual events: (1) gathering; (2) the creation of sacred space; (3) invocation; (4) purgation; (5) setting a central symbol; (6) calling in the new; (7) raising energy and affirmation; and (8) completion and commission. These elements will provide a structure for the description of each ritual.

Initially this book was conceived to cover eight celebrations, one for each turning of the season in the wheel of the year. That would include the winter and summer solstices, when the sun is at its highest and lowest points in the sky, and the spring and autumnal equinoxes, when day and night are equally balanced. Many cultures, from Celtic Irish to ancient Babylonian, also celebrated what are called the cross-quarter days, the days midway between the solstices and equinoxes, when the biosphere responds to the solar event that occurred six weeks earlier. These were the more important celebrations for grain-producing people, and I have included all of them here: Halloween or Samhain (chapter 3); Candlemas or Imbolc (chapter 5); May Day or Beltane (chapter 7); and the Festival of First Fruits or Lammas (chapter 8).

I have also included two feminist rites of passage as examples of rituals specifically for women as women. Much as we need to rebind ourselves to nature through seasonal celebrations, we have other passages too, based on social and personal events, which we need to mark. Sometimes these are simply on the occasion of a conference, as we see in the Seven-Gated Passage (chapter 9). Others are highly personal, like the one a friend asked me to help her design and lead, a rite of passage into womanhood for herself and all those women who had never felt themselves formally acknowledged as women (chapter 10). Both of these are explicitly feminist in purpose and content.

The rite of passage into womanhood described in chapter 10 was for women of mixed races and different faiths, from secular humanist to evangelical Christian. Many were of African American descent. None of the women at this gathering had significant formal knowledge of what would be called "women's spirituality." It was important to operate in a way that would be respectful of the differences in faith and culture yet genuinely empowering for all the women present from a feminist perspective. I include it because it used no sacred or Goddess symbols per se, yet was specifically designed as an empowerment ritual for a diverse group of women.

The ritual described in chapter 9, took place close enough to the autumnal equinox to call it an equinox ritual for the purposes of this writing. In fact I did it for a feminist spirituality conference called the Dance of Change, hosted annually by the Immaculate Heart Community Feminist Spirituality Program in Los Angeles. This community, in contrast with the community served by the Woman's Day Ritual, is commitedly feminist, largely or formerly Roman Catholic, and primarily white with a few women of color. Participants in this initiation were women who, whatever their level of experience with such things, had specifically chosen to attend a feminist ritual of transformation. Of all the rites included in this collection, I would say this was the most rigorous and demanding of the participants. According to later reports from participants, I believe it also worked as a rite of transformation.

In the seasonal rituals covered here, we begin turning the wheel of the year in chapter 3, Cauldron of Rebirth (Samhain), with a neo-Wiccan Halloween ritual, which I believe to be a good example of this style of ritual done well. It was performed with about thirty people who were members of a Neopagan church who circled together regularly, making their highest celebrations the cross-quarters of Halloween or Samhain, and its opposite pole, May Day or Beltane, which I cover in a later chapter. These two rites are offered as examples of nature spirituality rituals as they are being practiced, and adapted, today, in a single community. They are also the most obviously Wiccan in style of the rituals included here.

Chapter 7, Feminism Meets Fertility Rites (May Day), describes a feminist redesign of a traditional Maypole rite in that same community. The Maypole dance is still done today throughout the English-speaking world. Children crown the Virgin Mary with wreaths of flowers in churches, and dance with streamers around a pole to ring in the spring. The origins of these quaint customs are far more Pagan than most people realize. In pre-Christian Northern European tradition, the Maypole dance is a phallocentric fertility rite celebrating the sexual union of Goddess and God, as the earth bursts into bloom.

In this modern California version we return to the traditional Pagan form, but with a feminist twist. The phallocentricity of the rite raises the question of how to sensitize the phallus without cutting off the testicles, as a friend of mine delicately put it. My partner and I used the Maypole ritual as an occasion for ritual reeducation, celebrating the phallic Maypole as an instrument of pleasure rather than conquest, and symbolically placing its use in the hands of the women to determine when and how it would enter sacred space. I am told that the changes that we made to the ritual still are in effect in that community today.

Other rituals described here were performed with different groups. Both equinox rituals were performed inside the feminist spirituality community at

Immaculate Heart College Center, primarily for women. Chapter 6, Cakes for the Queen of Heaven (Spring Equinox), was designed for a public spring equinox gathering, followed by a four-day course on feminist ritual and liturgy. Because this ritual was designed as a teaching tool, the liturgical steps and explanations are especially clear, within the classic form. This is an explicitly feminist rite, with explicitly feminist intentions and purposes, in contrast to chapter 5, A Little Bit of Light (Candlemas), for example, in which the feminism is entirely implicit. "Cakes" is an example of a ritual engaging a large group of mostly inexperienced people, which is a particular kind of design and facilitation challenge. It is also a good example, I believe, of reclaiming myths and symbols for feminist ends

The final ritual in the wheel of the year series is chapter 9, Seven-Gated Passage (the autumnal equinox), performed in the same community of women. As mentioned above, it was actually designed for a feminist spirituality conference. But it was done in the autumn, close to the equinox, and fits the descent motif consistent with the season. The autumnal equinox is most frequently correlated to the harvest. It is a good time to take note of and give thanks for the fruits of the year's labors. This ritual, however, is related to another, less pleasant, aspect of nature's world at harvest time, namely, culling. In this ritual the women are asked to cull, or cut out, from their lives whatever will not aid them in building a feminist future. I am fond of it in part because it calls forth the fierce face of the Goddess, breaking the all too frequent stereotype of the Goddess as nurturer.

The ritual in chapter 4, Out of the Darkness (the winter solstice), was included as an example of a simple solstice service for a Unitarian fellowship, where members and ministers are regularly experimenting with seasonal ritual done in circle. One of the greatest gifts of the Wiccan and seasonal heritage is a theology that allows people to reclaim the darkness as a positive space or, in the words of feminist songwriter Frankie Armstrong, to "Take Back the Night." In this chapter I explore the thealogical import of doing so.

The ritual chosen for Candlemas (chapter 5, A Little Bit of Light) was designed and facilitated by a group of people who led monthly inspirational events at the Sufi house in San Rafael, California. I proposed to translate the Irish seasonal celebration of the returning light into a liturgical form more familiar and appropriate for Sunday-morning worship in a New Age community. I believe the experiment was successful. This critique grapples with whether feminist ritual can occur without being explicit.

No summer solstice ritual is represented in this book. Summer solstice has always seemed to me more appropriately commemorated by a beach party, or a picnic, than by a ritual. Later today (summer solstice '97) I will meet friends in their large backyard for barbecued salmon and pesto rice. We will eat salad from their garden. The children will play on the homemade water slide. I may call people together around the table and ask them each to toast the sun in thanksgiving for life and growing things on this planet. My partner will sing "Anthem to the Sun." Then we will eat and drink and celebrate the sun by being in it. Some rituals are implicit.

The penultimate seasonal ritual (chapter 9) represented here is probably the least-known cross-quarter day in today's world. It comes at the beginning of August and is called Lammas, or Loaf Mass. I call it the Festival of First Fruits. It marks the beginning of the end of summer, and the opening of the harvest season. It is traditionally a time for the making of offerings. The ritual I selected to write about here was a benefit concert in the park, constructed liturgically, to honor the season and encourage offerings from the audience. It is an interesting example of ritual as part of a large public event.

* NOT RECIPES BUT RITUALIZING *

I offer this broad array of styles and voices to make clear that the form and style of a rite must fit its purpose and be accessible to the participants, or it is useless. No single style will fit every situation and group. Therefore the rituals described in this book are not meant to be copied and reused as they are. They are offered merely as models. My intent is to encourage others, in their own explorations in their own traditions, to consciously ritualize and share their insights, and also to provide a critical framework for doing so.

I am more interested in bridging the gap between Christian and Goddess-centered feminists than I am in describing, theorizing about, or promoting rarefied and esoteric practices of any sort. I therefore offer this book as a resource to the many women (and more than a few men) both inside and outside the Christian tradition who are exploring new and empowering forms of feminist religious expression, as well as to Neopagans and the growing number of Unitarian Universalists exploring nature and Goddess-centered forms of worship. As women of all faith traditions reclaim our religious authority to use rite and symbol to empower ourselves and our sisters, we become strong enough to reshape the world.

The benefits of this symbolic reshaping could be enormous, not only for women, but for the life of the earth. Feminine symbols of the divine rooted in nature open the way for a scientifically credible, feminist panentheism, which could be the next step in a human understanding of our place in the world. Taking back symbolic language, probably invented by women, is no small thing.[12] If feminists are going to transform religious symbols and actions so that they are relevant, numinous, and empowering to all women, to aid us in creating the world we envision, we shall have to take ourselves seriously as shapers of symbolic reality. This will require us to own and hone our skills and to recognize the institutional patriarchal forces we challenge in doing so. Whoever holds the symbols, shapes the rituals, reflects the divine, has the power to define our internal and our external reality. She who rules the symbols rocks the world.

This book is offered as a tool for bringing feminism to public ritual and for empowering women in the creation of our common future. Nothing could be more important for the future of women on this planet.

REALITY IN THE SHAPE
OF A WOMAN

Some events, changes, and passages in life are beyond human ability to comprehend. Consider death. One moment I am holding someone's hand. I can feel its warmth. I can see the blood pulsing and feel this person's heart beating. I can observe the chest rising and falling rhythmically, as the breath moves in and out. Then in a moment, this all stops. No more breath, no more heartbeat. What was warm, breathing, moving, and changing—a person—is now still and cold—a corpse.

How does one explain this shift from the state of being alive to that of being dead? The cause of death—say cancer or old age—could be cited. The mechanics of how the heart stops pumping could be described. But such tactics hardly enable one to grasp the profound and simple fact that a person who laughed and cried and shared with us is no more.

Likewise, consider the seasons' passing. Only last week, I was frolicking on the beach, letting my skin turn brown. Today I feel a chill in the air, and I note with nostalgia that yesterday was the autumnal equinox, the first day of autumn. While I have a reasonable working knowledge of the way in which the earth moves about the sun and rotates on its axis, and the way in which a seed ripens under the ground, there is another level on which the passage of summer into autumn, or the rebirth of the year from winter into spring, is as much a mystery and a miracle to me today as it must have been to cave dwellers many thousands of years ago. The earth's journey is a mystery and a miracle beyond my ability to comprehend it.

Life is full of mysterious passages of various magnitudes: some are personal, others social, still others cultural. Some are even global. Many transitions operate in several spheres at the same time. It is the mystery innate within transitional events that prompts wonder and often ritual response. For example, even though knowledge of genetic reproduction is growing, it does not fully prepare us for the mystery of a new baby, born into a family and community. In some cultures wild celebration, fireworks, special foods and drink mark the baby's arrival. Some U.S. cultural practices reflect these when, for example, cigars are given out, announcements sent, baby showers hosted, and a baptism or naming ceremony enacted.

With each year's passing, marked by one birthday after another, I acquire more wisdom and more wrinkles. I blow out candles on a cake, and friends and family applaud. By this act I am ritually recognized for my passage into another year of life. This affirms my transition from one year to the next.

Two people who lived single lives yesterday today are considered a legal unit through a ceremony in which they declare their unity before their families and community. Although the ritualizations vary greatly from one culture to the next, and even from one couple to the next, marriage is still, in all societies, a highly ritualized occasion, probably because it marks a major life transition that occurs through declaration and agreement alone.

After years of hard work and angst, a person receives an official document that declares him or her qualified to practice in some field. A graduation ceremony marks the passage from student to practitioner or master.

A son's voice deepens as he suddenly shoots up three inches in height. A daughter's shape is changing, and she has her first menses. These young people have entered a new phase of life, open to the mysteries and the dangers of sex. Because socially accepted, effective rites of passage into the adult world are lacking for them, they will often devise their own, by smoking cigarettes, drinking alcohol, having sex, even joining a gang with its own initiation rites.

After forty-five years or more of work and saving, a person is at the stage called retirement, in which she or he will not have to work (or work as much) for a living any longer.

The trees that were bare only last week are sprouting buds that will soon flower.

The first asparagus of the season arrives at the vegetable market.

The first tomato of the year ripens in the garden.

The grapes are ready to press.

It is dark by 5:00 P.M., the longest night.

The earth heaves, wiping out entire villages filled with people and animals.

A loved one dies.

These events are just some of life's mysteries and passages—social, personal, and seasonal—that somehow remain unchanged by the age of computers and jet travel. They are at the heart of what it means to be human and alive in the world that we share. Although we may mark them in many different ways or not at all, they are nonetheless awesome and filled with mystery.

✳ ENGAGING THE UNKNOWN ✳

What is it that allows us to apprehend things that we cannot fully comprehend? How can we engage that which we cannot explain? The language of symbols is the best and first means that human beings have invented for relating to these mysteries. We affirm our commitment to another person through the symbolic exchange of rings. We bind ourselves to our country and its laws through pledging allegiance to its flag. Placing a symbolic handful or shovel full of dirt on the casket or scattering ashes helps us to accept a death. Lighting a candle helps us to remember someone who has died.

Through our relationship to symbols we make something coherent of our lives. We name and relate to that which we name, through its name. We have a relationship to that which has a name. It exists for us at a different level. It is differentiated, distinguished from the rest of the world. Likewise that which we symbolize. The developments of symbols and of language go hand in hand, all language being symbolic of a thing or idea. Symbolic reality creates shape and meaning.

By manipulating and interacting with symbols in a highly specific manner in a particular time and place, we act to accept, affirm, release, bind ourselves to, or alter a particular reality through our symbolic interaction with it. The frame or context in which we do these things is a ritual. Older than reason, ritual helps human beings grasp and traverse life's passages, integrating biological and cultural events at a level that reaches beneath the rational mind's ability to explain them.[1] Because ritual reaches into all three parts of the triune brain structure of humans, and works on both right and left hemispheres, it can reach beneath the cognitive to disseminate information on a precognitive level.[2] Through the use of repetition, rhythm, and shock, ritual engages reptilian, mammalian, and neocortical layers of the human brain. People are able to grasp events and information at a deeper and more embodied level, enabling them to incorporate the changed reality addressed by the rite, and go on with their lives.

Ritual "allows for the acquisition of much new knowledge, in paradigmatic and symbolic form." Such rites were very likely how Paleolithic people educated their younger members into full adulthood in the clan. They are still used in tribal societies for that purpose, in places where the tribe's survival depends on the education of the young into the ways and story of their people. Ritual shapes the fundamental meaning systems in a culture at a precognitive level, which precedes the rational. It forms the basis of what "feels right" or does not. Through repetition and surprise, it educates our hearts and bodies as to who we are and what our place is in the world.[3]

Ritual is far older and more basic to humans than any religion or theology. Neanderthals are thought to have placed flowers on the graves of their dead hundreds of thousands of years before what we now call civilization. The first human music ever made was probably the drumming and chanting where people gathered to celebrate the seasons, to pray or give thanks for a successful hunt, and to bind their lives to the mysterious turning of nature's wheel. The first art found on cave walls and pots and in burial sites was symbolic art, probably used in magic and ritual initiation. It is unlikely that Paleolithic people first sat around a fire theologizing about the nature of the universe or the meaning of life. No, they drummed and danced and went into trances and made symbolic actions in response to life's mysteries. They communed with the gods as they knew them. Their meaning systems were then taken from the enactment.[4]

Ritual comes first. The impulse to do it may be innate. "Everything points to the supposition that our remote ancestors were ritualizing before they became human. . . . Ritualization is the source also of speech, of religion, of culture, and of ethics. It is not as true to say that we humans have invented rituals as that rituals have invented us."[5] It is generally only after ritualizing that people seek to explain what they were doing through theologizing. People did not stop and consider whether or not God was female when they paid homage to the Great Mother; rather, as they saw all life being born to mothers, it seemed natural to them that the Great Mother would have given birth to all life.

* THE POWER TO NAME *

Why does it matter what we call that which we cannot fully know? Surely there is something beyond all our naming that does not care what we call it, only that we admire it and bask in its glory. In a world that celebrates diversity, it is important to honor the many different ways that people call and interact with the holy, by whatever name. As Gregory Bateson put, it, the map is not the territory, and our naming is merely the map. By the same token, what we find, even what we know to look for, is determined by the map we are using. I will not go looking for New Jersey if I do not know it exists.[6]

The manner in which we name or symbolize our ground of being defines the container through which we apprehend it and the lens through which we view it. True, what we point to when we speak of God is larger than any box we try to place around it and grander than any name we give it. It is neither man nor woman. However, our conceptions of it are described and circumscribed by what we call and how we symbolize it. If what we perceive is determined by the shape of the container in which we hold it, a male-shaped container for the sacred will forever place men in a superior position, and keep women in the role of the "other." "If God in 'his' heaven is a father ruling his people, then it is the nature of things and according to divine plan and the order of the universe that society be male-dominated."[7] It is clear, then, that it is not peripheral to women's cause to radically transform the ritual and symbol system of the culture. It is pivotal.

Human beings seem to have a built-in mechanism for creating meaning. We are nature's storytellers. In my class in feminist liturgy and ritual I passed around a basket covered by a cloth. In the basket were five objects with symbolic portent: an egg, a mirror, a snakeskin, a sand dollar, and a knife. I asked my students to each silently raise the cloth, examine the contents, and write down the meaning of what they saw. Each student wrote a set of meanings slightly different from the next. Some wove the symbols together to form a story.

All of these objects have archetypal content, yet none has intrinsic meaning. They are merely a collection of objects. The meaning is added. It is what we give them. It is this added meaning, not the object itself, that shapes our understandings in a particular manner. The meanings accrete over time, with a patina added each time they are used in a ritual setting. A chalice is just a glass if I am thirsty; an egg is just an egg when I make an omelet. Yet place the same egg on an altar, and it becomes a symbol of new life, of hope and birth. It points to something larger and more multilayered than we could describe with a few words. An ordinary loaf of bread broken in a communion rite takes on the resonance of all the rituals in which people have broken bread together. The meaning and the action together are archetypal, yet they are not innate in the bread: rather they are intrinsic to our association to the bread. There is more depth to this action, and more meaning, than we could express in mere words. A symbol is always more than what we can say in words. That is why we use the symbol.

The meaning we get from a symbol depends on the meaning attached to it by the culture. If I were in ancient Crete a snake would portend magic and transformation; if I am a fundamentalist Christian it symbolizes evil and temptation. Depending on which of these meaning/symbol systems has shaped my reality, I will react to the snake accordingly, probably without knowing why, thinking it is normal, thinking I am responding to the snake itself, rather than to the meaning attached to it.

A symbol stirs something deep within us either because it calls forth something that is intrinsic to us by our nature as human beings, or through its repeated use in the culture. Certain symbols are probably universal, being nature based, like flowers. Others, like the cross, are culture based, evoking a response from those acculturated in a particular meaning system. An example of this is the Coke bottle that fell from the sky in the film *The Gods Must Be Crazy*. For the people in the movie, the bottle acquired symbolic meaning to which only they would respond. We must not think, however, that symbols can be invented out of whole cloth. I cannot put a flat tire on an altar and declare it a symbol for failed dreams. It would remain merely anecdotal, stirring nothing deeper than amusement or shock, pointing to nothing larger than itself. Lacking numinosity, patina, and depth, it could not rightfully be called a symbol, but only a sign.

Symbol and story organize our thought forms and culture in much the same way as our DNA organizes our bodies. They provide the categories for sorting information. Without them everything is random. For the most part we cannot perceive what exists outside our symbolic framework. If a concept shows up for which we have no context, it falls through the cracks of our brain. People who have many different words for different types of snow actually perceive different kinds of snow, which I, lacking the language, do not. In some important way, language and symbols are all human beings have. Out of the ways in which we symbolize reality, we organize our world. Our symbols, while not pretending to embody ultimate truth, make all the difference in the world.

* FEMINIST SYMBOL MAKING *

The realm of symbol and story—disseminated through ritual—influences the shape of human reality. Feminists daring a vocation of mainstream symbol making have an opportunity to reshape the world according to feminist values. To do so we shall have to wrest the symbols from the hands of the patriarchy and transform or replace them with symbols that empower women. This means appropriating the myths and archetypes that shape consciousness. Transforming the rituals that transmit the symbols that tell us who we are, it is possible to introduce a feminist view into the world at a precognitive level.

Claiming Women's Power

According to Mary Collins, "Feminist liturgy aims to explore and celebrate a new order of ultimate relationships, one that is saving or redemptive insofar as it heals the destructive disorder wrought by patriarchal consciousness."[8] An empowering, female image of the divine is key to that redemption. It is not enough to de-sex God. What feminists need is not to castrate male power but to claim female power. Religious imagery has too long known God as male for gender-neutral language to suffice to replace that image in our imaginations. There is little power in neutered language; it remains too abstract to grab onto viscerally, for a primary experience of the sacred. In the end we are left with nothing but a castrated JHWH, placid and manageable like any castrato, but missing all the wildness and strength we sense and need in a greater power.

Women need an image of the divine who is a reflection of all that has been rejected about the female in patriarchal religion. The Virgin Mary will not do as a stand-in for the multidimensional Goddess. She is too tame, too sweet, too easily turned to ends designed to subordinate women. Obedient to men and a male god, she provides the patriarchal model for "good" women: mothers and virgins.

The Goddess is fleshy, carnal, immanent, fierce, powerful, autonomous, wild, transforming, and natural, as well as nurturant, giving, abundant, and comforting. She holds the power of death and decay in her body, as well as the power of life and birth. She is solar as well as lunar.[9] Her embrace covers the sky as well as the earth. She is divine mind as well as divine body. She is woman identified and defined. She is primary and essential. She is generative. She is an archetype, not a stereotype, and she may not always be "feminine" in the common usage of the word.

Like a snake gone opaque
She hides in the jungles of the chromosome
She lies at the hydrocarbon's heart
She is the black hole itself
Between Her thighs
The universe is squeezed from spirit.[10]

Feminist Spirituality and the Feminine

This is where feminist spirituality veers sharply from some trends in women's spirituality. Women's spirituality is too often rooted in a male-defined notion of the "feminine" and of woman. Feminist spirituality is rooted in feminist analysis and theology in its treatment and image of women. It puts forward a critique, implicit or explicit, of patriarchal religion. Feminist spirituality stands for women's religious, social, and political emancipation and power. Its fulfillment would result in the freedom, actualization, and fulfillment of all women.

What then is meant by "the feminine"? A great deal of literature talks of "the feminine" and "the masculine" as if these were real things, actual boxed sets of qualities set to swoop down from Jungian heaven at the birth of a boy or a girl baby. Yet, despite a proliferation of research on sexual dimorphism in everything from language to brain functioning, the question of what, if anything, is intrinsically masculine or feminine beyond our actual biological sexual characteristics remains open to investigation. We just don't know enough yet to state clearly if there are authentically sex-linked characteristics that are entirely innate.

Margaret Mead and Ruth Benedict demonstrated long ago that, while all societies have distinct notions of what is masculine or feminine behavior, the content of these definitions varies widely from culture to culture. For example, in Victorian England, it was a culturally accepted "fact" that men had a greater sex drive and interest than women. Yet in the Arab world, women were—and are—believed to have the greater sex drive. Sexual energy was described as a masculine or feminine quality accordingly. In both cases the phenomenon was observably true. Yet clearly, in at least one of the positions, it was a social artifact. Likewise, logic and business sense are said to be, alternately, women's domain or men's, depending upon the cultural norm.[11]

Nevertheless there is a persistent set of qualities that are cross-culturally defined as "feminine" as opposed to "masculine." These are characteristics that transcend particular sex roles and embody essential qualities said to be feminine. These are the qualities referred to as archetypal. But where do they come from? Is there, as Plato suggested, an unchanging ideal or archetypal realm in which "the essential feminine" and "the essential masculine" can be said to reside, preexisting unchanging, and informing the material realm? Is this realm one in which the Great Dealer (no doubt male) distributes human qualities like cards in the archetypal card game? Does he divvy up the human qualities so that we all have some of both, but well-adjusted women have more of one kind (feminine) and men have more of the other (masculine)? Is it a fifty-fifty split? Was it different before Jung discovered his anima? Did men have the entire masculine repertoire then, while women had all the feminine? And while we're at it, what are these qualities? Are they an even hand, or do some trump others?

Giving even cursory attention to sources from I Ching to Jungian psychology, the wisdom of the ages tells us that man does; woman is. The masculine is the positive, active energy; the female is the receptive. The masculine is light; the feminine is darkness. The masculine is the sun (illumination, or generative light); the feminine is the moon (reflected light). The masculine represents consciousness; the feminine is the unconscious. The masculine rules the realm of thought, while the feminine is said to rule emotion and intuition. Men embody the creative principle; women embody nurturance. Man acts; woman is acted upon. Man is spirit; woman is matter. So the feminine is thought to embody darkness, the unconscious, the material, the receptive characteristics undervalued in the culture, the murky primordial realm from which civilization arose and must continue to transcend.

Upon examination, these attributes do not seem to be randomly dealt. The so-called masculine qualities are those designed to keep men in power. They are the subject qualities, the qualities that empower autonomy, generativity, and creativity. They are valued in our world. The so-called feminine qualities of receptivity, on the other hand, valuable though they are, are not self-generating or initiatory. They are object qualities. Existing only in relationship to the masculine, they can once again be said to put women in a position of "otherness." While society needs to reclaim these darker qualities for spiritual balance, let us separate them from gender. Attributing them to the feminine could consign women to a position of passivity that would keep us "in the dark" for another thousand years or so.

This gendered essentialism rising within the women's spirituality movement comes dangerously close to resurrecting the Gnostic spirit/matter dichotomy, in which the divine and natural worlds are separate, and in which the masculine stands for the active spirit needed by the feminine to animate her inert matter. It only confuses the issue to claim that women are endowed with an "inner masculine" and men with an "inner feminine." Such notions simply hold in place our stereotyped, and male-defined, images. Moreover, such rationalizations obfuscate the obvious "ghost in the machine" metaphysic of spirit/ matter, in which the so-called male principle is the spirit, or (no doubt holy) ghost, and the so-called female principle is the matter, or (you guessed it) the machine.[12]

Feminist Consciousness versus Soft Power

The notion of an inner feminine possessed by men places both women and nature in the position of being passively acted upon, or animated, by male-spirit. Its reintroduction within a Goddess-worshiping subculture is none the less dangerous. More insidiously, it may perpetuate the very system of male and female selves critiqued by Catherine Keller, in which "to have a 'feminine' soul allows (the dominant male) to keep his ego in control and on top of his holdings in the world, while tapping the underground fluids of the psyche: the best of both worlds, without their mutual transformation."[13] One is reminded of Zeus swallowing Metis so that she might forever give him her wise counsel from inside his belly. Indeed, he was in touch with his "inner feminine."

This language should raise a red flag for feminists. As feminists give way to Nouvelle Jungians in the movement to reclaim the Goddess, her wholeness could be reduced. Without a feminist consciousness, the Goddess can become merely the internal feminine archetype, the all-giving, self-sacrificing mommy of our infant dreams, or a sort of sexually active Virgin Mary. These images, put forward by a noncritical Neopagan or women's spirituality movement, easily become expectations made of women. This does not serve the cause of women's emancipation or empowerment.

Alas, even rituals of the Goddess can disempower women, if we use them without a feminist critique and without a clear commitment to all women, as women of the suttee would no doubt warn us. It all depends on whether we allow narrow, patriarchal, male-created definitions of the feminine to circumscribe our ideas about her. Unless women are vigilant in insisting that archetype not be confused with stereotype, Goddess worship will just become more grist for the patriarchal mill, as happened long ago in patriarchal Greece and Rome and continues today in India.[14]

Let us remember that Carl Jung, visionary though he was, was a white, Swiss, Victorian man. It cannot serve the interests of women to defer to him or any other man as the last word on the divine feminine. If women allow Jung to be the source of authority for the new ground we are breaking in the realm of spirituality and religion, we may find ourselves back on the old, familiar ground of "soft power" promoted by women's magazines in the 1950s. Women risk identifying themselves and their deity with a stereotyped set of male-defined "feminine" or receptive characteristics, which can be used to reinforce sex roles (or which men can lay equal claim to, in their appropriation of the Goddess movement). The patriarchy will grind out ever more subtle and insidious propaganda on the soft power of the inner feminine as an obfuscation of the same old saw of the woman behind the man. Some men will begin to claim, as I heard one do, that equal representation of women in positions of authority is of no consequence, so long as the men are in touch with their "inner feminine."

Personally, I trust nature more than I trust psychiatry. If there is any basis for the notion of a feminine, it is to biology, as a systematic reading of nature's tendencies and proclivities, that we should turn. This physical, biological force has little to do with ancient or current metaphysical notions of masculine and feminine principles. Nor does it correspond to the gendered essentialism currently being popularized by Jungian psychology, in spite of an unfortunate tendency to confuse the two. It is rooted in the natural world.

From this perspective, then, can we speak of the divine feminine? Surely there is no such thing, as a *thing*. But as the primary generative force of the universe, I would shout yes. A force does exist, a process in the living universe that is generative, birthing itself again and again in multiple variations. Anything that can reproduce itself is, by biological definition, female. The divine feminine is the sine qua non of biological existence on this planet, and it is far from passive.

This is not to place the feminine in a position of superiority. Superiority and inferiority are concepts superfluous in nature, where life exists in whole interdependent systems. It is to claim primacy, however, for the female as life giver. It is she who is unto herself, for it is she alone who can create life. This is simply to say there is no life on earth without reproduction and birth, and there is no reproduction and birth without the female. The Goddess is the creator and transformer immanent in nature, that mysterious regenerative process known as evolution, by which life creates, destroys, and re-creates itself.

With the introduction of external genetic material come death and difference. This is the biological contribution of the male to evolution. His action is catalytic. He is nature's wild card, which allows life to evolve and transform. I believe there must be room in feminist symbol making for the God, the counterpart and equal of the Goddess, as embodiment and sire of that force and process. Moreover, if we do not honor the primal masculine in our symbolizing, men will be forced to remain linked to patriarchal symbol systems of male dominance in order to see themselves reflected in the visage of the divine.

❋ FEMINIST CRITICISM OF RITUALIZING ❋

The following invocations reflect the bio-thealogical distinction between masculine and feminine as I understand them. The reader will note in the first invocation the primacy and wholeness of the force that is being described. This divine feminine cannot be tamed.

INVOCATION OF THE GODDESS

Canto:
She is the Mother
She is the Lover
She is the Dancer . . .
And . . .
She is the Devourer
Through her body all things are made new

Response:
O Lady, give us new life!
Canto:
She gives
And she takes away
She is the storehouse laden with grain
She is the famine-ridden land
And she is the rain
She flows in mountain streams and rivers
Her heart beats in the primordial seas' ebb and flow
She is the sandy river bottom blown away on summer's wind
    and the starry skies spinning constellations
And swallowing them whole
Through her body all things are made new

Response:
O Lady, give us new life!

Canto:
She is all into all
She is our wildest dreams
And our worst nightmares
She is all in all
We ride her tail like a dragon
She is all unto all
She is before all
And she is after all
Through her body all things are made new

Response:
O Lady, give us new life![15]

The second invocation of the God is to a wounded God. Many men are estranged from the Goddess out of fear they will lose their independence. This invocation calls them home, calls even the Judeo-Christian God to give up the masculine false pride and pretense of being the sole creator of life.

INVOCATION OF THE WOUNDED GOD

O wounded God, come home
How much longer must you wander in your fear and pride?
Don't you know that you are part of me?
You are my wildest dream and my worst nightmare
You are difference, my ecstatic whim
Wounded God, come to me
Be my sweetness and surprise
Take me where I would never venture alone
Touch me
Change me
Let me feel your galloping hooves vibrating across my damp meadow
Your crash of thunder, your flash of fire
Inundate my banks with your rushing waters
Blow your pollen deep into my waiting blossom
Come, wounded one, come, foolishness
Place your kiss of madness upon my lips
Your bloodroot thick with yearning between my thighs
Fear not
Be the tender stroke upon my cheek
The sweetness in my breast
And I shall call your name Pleasure
And I shall call you home.[16]

While the reemergence of the Goddess could be a cornerstone of women's empowerment, it could equally well be another means by which women are kept in their place, told to be sweet and nurturant, to carry more of the "feminine archetype." Patriarchy will use every weapon in its—and our—arsenal to prevent women's power from gaining a foothold. If its agents can reclaim feminine deity to their favor, they will do so, and they will have the help of many women, in the name of reconciliation, in the name of "balance." If they cannot wipe out all memory of the Goddess, they will try to tame her, and us, and all the wild, fecund and fetid, unmanageable, holy life that whispers her name.

Feminist criticism of ritualizing, then, begins with and remains focused on this basic point. An image of the divine feminine is not in itself assurance of women's emancipation. Nor is Goddess worship intrinsically or automatically empowering to women. They are not even automatically feminist. The potential remains for reifying nature and objectifying the Goddess, to appropriate her powers, tame her, and use her for patriarchal purposes. In contrast, if women recognize and honor the Goddess in all her aspects and changes—as did our most ancient and gynocentric forebears—and if we honor her solar as well as her lunar persona, warrior as well as midwife, devourer and virgin (woman-for-herself) as well as mother and lover, then perhaps our love of her will give us the strength we need to continue to fight for the freedom and dignity of all women and all life, as embodiments of her.[17]

In reshaping symbolic reality, women have the power to transform the world. Symbol and story are mutable forms, ready to be shaped by the hands of those who wield them artfully. Symbols and archetypes are not static; they live and breathe and change and transform as we interact with them. Symbols are living reflections of human religious experience. As we reclaim the world of symbolic language for our own purposes, we claim the power to enter it and alter its future.

Part
2

Celebrating Her

THE CAULDRON OF REBIRTH

✳

Halloween

The wheel begins its turning not with flowers and springtime, but with death and decay. It is the first weekend in November, time once again to enter the ancient, sacred circle of death and rebirth. This is the time of year when the days are noticeably shorter, and the realization is suddenly unavoidable: winter is coming. The sunsets burn orange against a strangely dark sky. In the secular culture of the United States, we know this time as Halloween, from the British All Hallows' Eve. The Mexican people celebrate it as Dia de los Muertos, or Day of the Dead. The Roman Catholic, Anglican, and Lutheran Churches call it All Souls' Day. Samhain ("summer's end," pronounced "Sow´-wen") is the Celtic name for this holy day honoring the year's entrance into the winter cycle of death and darkness.

According to all these traditions, this is the time, when the year is dying, that the veil between the worlds is thinnest, the time when we honor and communicate with our dead. It is one of the two highest holy days in the Wiccan and Neopagan calendars, the other being Beltane, or May Day, which ushers in the summer cycle of fertility and new birth. Samhain is the most solemn holiday of the Neopagan calendar. It is the new year, when trees drop their seeds before the winter frost to wait in darkness for germination. Therefore it is the time we lay down the seeds of what we wish to see taking root in the coming year. This ritual is a recognition of the core bio-thealogical principle that light and life emerge from death and darkness.[1]

I feel I have entered this circle (for every circle is the same circle) thousands of times past. My genes remember. My bones remember. As I robe (warmly, for we shall be outside for most of the night), I have a sense of timelessness, of deep connection to my ancestral roots. For did not our ancestors—native peoples of Europe, Africa, the Americas, the fertile crescent of the Middle East, and Asia—gather in circle to mark the passages in their lives and in the earth's cycles, for thousands of years before the coming of the missionaries and invaders?[2]

Archeological evidence indicates that nine thousand years ago masked, feathered priestesses danced funereal rites around the interred bones of their dead in circle at Çatal Hüyük, a Paleolithic village in what is now Eastern Turkey. Thousands of years and miles away, pre-Celtic peoples circled their observances of sun and earth cycles surrounded by the mysterious stones of Stonehenge and Avesbury, in Neolithic Britain. Indigenous peoples still do so, hidden from the eyes of official religion, on the mountain peaks of Peru and the islands of the South Seas. So we, too, gather to honor our passage through the wheel of the year, in the manner of our ancestors. My body remembers this.[3]

The rite described herein took place at the land sanctuary of the first officially incorporated Neopagan church in North America, now in its thirtieth year. For nearly a decade I cast the ancient circle with this motley tribe of Goddess worshipers at least twice every year—in the spring and in the fall—to mark through ritual the passing of the seasons; to reaffirm our connection to the divine and the connection of our own lives to the cycles of nature. There are women and men together in this circle, made up of predominantly white heterosexual and bisexual adults between the ages of thirty-five and fifty-five. Often, though not always, there are a few children present, and a scattering of teenagers, with their parents. Members are writers, welfare mothers, teachers, therapists, poets, students, computer programmers, healers, professionals, paraprofessionals, environmental activists, clerical workers, small-business owners, musicians, craftspeople, and scientists. There is a mix of rural and urban dwellers. Most are voracious readers, and although the level of formal education is unremarkable, the level of self-education and overall intellect is generally quite high.

The adults in the group were raised in a variety of traditions and none at all. Backgrounds include Roman Catholic, born-again Christian, mainline Protestant, Christian Scientist, Jewish, Mormon, and humanist. Some rebelled against the religions of their childhood as the result of deep wounding. Others simply moved on, out of a longing that was not being satisfied, or out of irreconcilable differences with their childhood faith. For the most part the participants are serious about their religion and, once becoming committed, remain so.

Some of the members of this group have been circling together thirty years. The ritual style that has evolved over that time derives from a highly creative synthesis of old European and Native American spirituality, Druidic tradition, Wicca, psychedelic experience, science fantasy, ancient texts and myths, feminist spirituality, environmental activism, naturalism, humanistic psychology, the new physics, Western esoteric occultism, and Eastern mystical traditions, and our own deep longings and intuitions of the sacred.

The group refers to itself as Neopagan, after the term *paganus* (peasant or country dweller), originally used to describe the rural people who continued to worship the old nature deities long after most Roman subjects had been converted to Christianity. The "neo" is because we realize full well that we neither can, nor wish to, re-create whole the nature religions of the past. Rather, we weave ourselves into a living tradition, as we augment, re-create, reinterpret, and transfigure ancient patterns in the light of today's world through our own needs and imaginations. Although it is difficult to measure, some estimates say that Neopaganism is the fastest-growing religion in America, its numbers having doubled from an estimated one hundred thousand in 1985 to two hundred thousand in 1989, according to author and National Public Radio journalist Margot Adler.[4]

Because this is a nature-based religion, most of the rituals take place out-of-doors. From Halloween until May Day, winter's darkness is emphasized and celebrated by holding rituals at night around a fire. In the warmer weather the group can be found dancing its rites in garden or meadow or at water's edge, glorifying the sun's warmth and light. Major celebrations often last all or most of the night, and sometimes into the next day, with between thirty and a hundred people in the circle.

A woman and a man are chosen each season by the church leadership (registered in the state of California) to be the worship designers and leaders, or priestess and priest, for that season's ritual. These two people engage the active participation of the general congregation in a variety of ways, often with additional people selected in advance to lead particular segments of the ritual.

Because of the vast amount of planning and work involved in developing an original rite of this size and scope, ritual leadership tends to rotate. Seldom will the same priestess or priest preside at two holidays in succession. This allows for a wide range of liturgical styles to coexist, some more formal, some more spontaneous, some more verbal, and some more kinesthetic or auditory. A.J., for example, uses harps, flutes, choreographed movement, and rhyming couplets in rituals often based on ancient esoteric systems describing and/or intervening in cosmic patterns. R.D.H. favors few words and lots of hypnotic chanting and drumming. Storytelling and song prevail at O.S's rituals, while O.Z. and M.G. love to reenact myth in an ancient form called the mystery play. I myself tend to focus on global concerns with a prophetic tone and a rock 'n' roll beat, while D.J.'s style is more pastoral, focusing on issues of personal transformation. While all this might seem a bit confusing at first (and I admit to preferring some styles to others aesthetically), ultimately I think it a good thing to have no "one true right and only way." It keeps things from ossifying. Ritual remains infused with meaning because it is constantly in the process of being shaped and reshaped. Just like life!

Still, there are certain givens that remain more or less constant. These forms give consistency and coherence to shared experience. Symbols become numinous only with continued use, gaining in value as each accretion of meaning adds to their patina. Their repeated use allows resonance to develop and deepen, along with the lived experience of the basic tenets that make up any religion.

This tradition's major symbols include the ever-turning wheel of seasons of the year, the four directions (north, east, south, and west) with their corresponding four elements (earth, air, fire, and water), the marriage of God and Goddess, the dying and reborn God (dying in the fall to be reborn in the returning light with the new greenery), and the triple goddess (maiden, mother, and crone). The basic ritual structure consists of casting a circle, calling on the four directions/elements, invoking Goddess and God, doing the ritual business that is to be done, raising power, grounding the power, communion, announcements and sharing, thanking God and Goddess, dismissing the four elements/directions, then opening the circle.

* THE RITUAL *

The ritual I am examining here was performed in November of 1991 by a group of which I was a part for nearly a decade, for its internal Halloween, or Samhain, celebration. I selected it for inclusion from among many Samhain rituals I have led or attended for three reasons: (1) It illustrates fundamental theological concepts in Neopagan practice and clearly illustrates the differences from Christian views of male and female deity, transcendence and immanence, light and darkness, death and rebirth, and the human place in nature. (2) It is the most traditionally Wiccan of the rituals included in this book, which have departed from this form as they have evolved. (3) Notably, I had nothing to do with the planning or leadership of this ritual, so I can be more objective in my evaluation.

Gathering, Creating Sacred Space, and Invoking

The ritual begins after dark, with half an hour of silence. Then thirty of us (all adults except for three adolescents who have completed their rites of passage, and one insistent girl of eleven, with her mother) process, single file, across a rickety wooden bridge under a big tree, into a circle that is sheltered from wind by a tall fence. The circle is cast by the priestess, who walks around the circumference chanting:

"Magic, magic everywhere, in the earth and in the air, how to hold the magic here? How raise it up and bring it down?"

She returns to the north altar, and seals the circle with the vow of perfect love and perfect trust. "By the earth that is her body," she pronounces, holding up a rock. Then she raises her chalice of water and spills some upon the ground, saying, "By the water that is her womb and her flowing blood." She lights a candle so that it flares, and vows, "By the fire that is her quickening spirit." Finally, fanning the air broadly and spinning with a bird's wing, she says, "By the air that is her sacred breath," declaring our circle cast.

The elements of air, fire, water, and earth are called forth by members of the congregation. Then the priest steps forward and evokes the Goddess as wise woman/crone into the priestess. The priestess is well-chosen. She is a gray-haired woman recently croned, having lost her mother and begun her menopause. She is a psychotherapist by profession. She removes her ritual cloak to reveal a purple running suit beneath it. She comments humorously on the pleasures of being a modern crone, dressed for comfort, and ready for action. She is obviously comfortable in her body. Her voice is clear and natural, easy to listen to.

The priestess then evokes the lord of the underworld into the priest, who is, appropriately enough, a geologist by profession. He is beseeched to overcome his shyness, to remove his helmet of invisibility and preside over our ceremonies as he presides over his own realm of departed souls. The congregation follows the invocations with a chant which invites the dark lord to guide us "down in the darkness, where we go alone . . . where we cry our tears . . . where we face our fears."

Another priestess takes the circle now, one who is experienced in such matters, to lead the next section of the rites: welcoming the beloved dead. She invites us, one by one, to call out the names of those we would have with us, rebuking us to leave those who would be uncomfortable at such an event. The litany begins: Gene Roddenberry, Bill Graham, Dr. Seuss, Miles Davis, friends and relatives lost to AIDS and other illness, Iraqi children, plants and wildlife as well as human life lost in the Oakland Hills fire, all dead this year; then those friends, lovers, teachers, and family members we still remember and mourn: Gwydion, whose ashes are scattered on this land he left us seven years ago. We add the names of those long dead whose inspiration we seek in these times: Hypatia, librarian of Alexandria, Martin Luther King, Gandhi, Crooked Fox Woman, Elizabeth Cady Stanton, Margaret Sanger, Chief Seattle, Emma Goldman, Enheduanna. These are hard times and we need a lot of inspiration. We call on our foremothers and guides. At last, after nearly half an hour of naming, the priestess rings a bell, inviting those named to break bread with us in silence. As we pass around specially prepared food, we feel a sense of communion with those named. This completes the first section of the ritual.

Reflections

We meet in a circle, symbol of the wheel of the year and leveler of hierarchy and difference. It is no accident that this is the same form that feminists have used for group meetings and consciousness raising. There is no face-off of laity and clergy here; we are celebrants together. When we enter the circle, it is said that we enter a "world between the worlds," a sacred, liminal space where it is possible to enter into communion with the divine, step into the mythic, and actually alter the fabric of reality, if we enter it with perfect love and perfect trust.

Our circle, like the circles of many of the indigenous traditions we have encountered in our research, has four orientation points describing its circumference: north, south, east, and west, usually with an altar placed at each point. We begin by calling or invoking the four elements, the basic stuff of which life is made, into our circle, identifying and situating each element in its particular, appropriate geographical direction, depending on our locale. Because this community lives in Northern California, they identify the element of water with the Pacific Ocean, and so place water in the west. They call forth fire from the warmer south, and air from the east, bastion of airy intellect. They situate earth in the cold, rocky north, according to Celtic tradition. (In Maine or New York, this would all be different, of course, because there would be a large body of water to the east.)

It is clear from the first spoken words of this ceremony that we hold all of life as sacred: "Magic, magic everywhere, in the earth and in the air." We are not trying to get someplace else. It is clear that deity is here, embodied in air and rocks, in water and fire, in female and male persons. Our priestess and priest are easy in their roles. It is all very human. We are sanctifying our life on earth, not in order to gain some reward elsewhere, but for the purpose of aligning ourselves with that magic, putting ourselves and our lives in the flow of divine will. Tears and laughter have a place in our liturgy. We do not fear the expression of feeling. Our practice is fleshy. We celebrate the privilege of being alive and embodied.

There is one more piece of liturgical business that must be completed before moving to the substance of the particular celebration or working that has brought the group together: that of calling forth and recognizing the presence and assistance of deity: invoking. In our tradition that means invoking the female, generative, life-giving force we call the Goddess, (usually done by the female leader), and her consort, the God, (usually called by the male). Having put these pieces in place we may proceed to the particulars of the given ritual. Before we "open the circle" at ritual's end, to return to chronological or secular time, we must remember to thank those forces whose attendance we requested by our invocations.

Purgation, Defining a Central Symbol, and Raising Power

The next section of the ritual is this year's version of a fine old new year's tradition: letting go of the old to make room for the growth of the new. This is the main order of business at this time of year, as the trees are shedding the last of their leaves. There can be no room for new growth without emptying out. Because purgation is the main business, the cauldron becomes the central symbol of this ritual.

Upon our return to the circle we find Hecate sitting in its center, her features shrouded by a dark scarf and cloak, stirring a cauldron on her lap. Though we know this person as our friend and priestess, for us in this moment she is Hecate, the Greek version of the ancient crone goddess, reclaimer of lost and broken souls. She is the wise woman, able to see into all our dark secrets. She is kind.

There is no need for harshness. There is nothing to hide. She is introduced with "The Crone Song," sung by its author, accompanying herself on guitar:

Come to us now, Great Queen of the Heavens
Kali, Binah, Hecate
We dance your circle in pairs and sevens
And ask your magic to show us the way
To begin
this difficult transformation
From within
We chant your invocation
Come to us now, Grandmother Crone
We call you home.[5]

She is here. Hecate takes the circle. She tells us what she has come for, what she can offer us: "Now is the sacrifice of souls, now is the giving up, the stripping down to the bone. The time of bones is the time of no compromise. Throw it all into Hecate's soup, let her stir it up, and we shall see what will be born anew. Come," she invites us, indicating her cauldron, "throw it in. This is the womb of rebirth, the cup of immortality. Give yourselves freely. Do not hold back. This is the moment. I can use it all. Oh, what a spicy soup this will be!"

Last year's May king (see chapter 7 for explanation) begins by offering his crown as a symbolic sacrifice for all the life that comes to an end in the winter, that it might in exchange be reborn in the spring. One by one we step forward and place ourselves before her, addressing her for all to hear. By our own volition, we offer dysfunctional and worn-out parts of ourselves and our lives to be composted in her cauldron of rebirth.

We feel the weight of old habits and attitudes dropping from our shoulders. What relief that she will take them! We offer self-doubts and self-hatreds, addictions, self-deceptions, and self-sabotage, fears, prides, shames, all into the soup. A welfare mother says she wants to give up poverty. A child gives up the pretense to perfection. A timid young woman throws in her fear of saying what she thinks. I feel the girdle around my soul growing tighter.

I walk toward the cauldron, unsure exactly what I will say. "I have grown so small and tight," I begin, "I have become so negative, so bitter, I hardly recognize myself." She beckons me forward. "I want to give you my rage, my suspiciousness. I find I am looking at everybody with suspicion. I have built a shell around myself, and I can't even laugh or love freely anymore." I place my head on her lap and begin to sob.

"Yes, that's it," she assures me gently. She strokes my hair and invites me to place my head over the cauldron and put it all in. A roar forms in my belly, catches in my throat, then tears its way out through my vocal chords. I feel the tightness leaving me. The bitterness so long with me begins to evaporate. I feel able to breathe for the first time in years. I am released. "Thank you, Grandmother," I whisper, before returning to my spot in the circle.

The letting-go continues at its own pace, peppered with wise comments from Hecate about nature's ways of breaking down even the most stubborn of substances. It is all grist for her mill, food for her worms. This is not the tragedy of life, but a part of its mystery. We take our time. We have all night.

The ritual moves on. We are asked to name those things that have been taken from us against our will which are already in the cauldron. This year has been a hard one for many in the group. One member lost in the Oakland fire her home, her extensive art and mythology library, and her book in progress. Another lost her brother-in-law, her cat, her son's grandfather, and the hard drive in her computer, all in the same week. One member's marriage dissolved. Several members lost jobs and economic security. We say goodbye to all that has been shattered and lost, never to return, and release it, along with our suffering, to Hecate's cauldron of changes. "Cauldron of changes, blossom of bone, arc of eternity, hole in the stone," we chant.[6]

Now for the final ingredients: What would we like to see go back to its elemental beginnings to compost, releasing its energy to be used for something new? Here the ritual moves from the personal to the planetary. Our personal material is already in the soup. What needs to decay in our larger world and system for life, love, and liberation to prevail? We stand and form our hands and bodies into a DNA spiral in reverse.

We are a wand of decomposition. We move as one (counterclockwise for unwinding) to the altar of each element and call out the names of things we wish to see disintegrate: rigid stances, unforgiving self-righteous attitudes, greed, corruption, nuclear weapons, clear-cutting of forests, addictions, the budget for building more highways, John Sununu's job, acid rain, rape, hatred of women, hatred of men, sloppy thinking, lies, "airy-fairy" ungroundedness, battering, child abuse, pollution, the AIDS virus. Be gone! "Down, down, decomposing, recomposing." Our voices get louder, our energy grows more intense, and our movement faster as we banish all this to the compost heap with our chant. The magic is done.

R e f l e c t i o n s

The natural cycle of life (decomposition, dormancy, conception, gestation, birth, growth, reproduction, maturation, decomposition) provides a language and paradigm which lend depth to our work, when used well, as occurred in the section of Hecate's cauldron, where we were dealing with predominantly personal material. In a nature-centered paradigm, rather than confessing to a transcendent god, then being granted absolution through penance or grace, people shed parts of themselves and their lives to be decomposed and recomposed. Nothing is ever lost to the Goddess. It is important to realize, however, that this ritual moment is effective in the transformation of sin and/or suffering only if it takes place in the context of repentance, in its original meaning: to turn around and walk the other way. The cauldron can only transform what one genuinely releases to it.

When all who wish to have added their ingredients to Hecate's soup, it is time for us to personally enter the underworld. This is said to be the night of all the year when we can best complete old business, reclaim lost memories or reintegrate exiled parts of ourselves. Our priest induces a trance state and takes those of us who wish to follow down past layers of humus, rock, molten lava, down a dark narrow corridor, into our own unconscious. We find ourselves in a setting our conscious minds may have long forgotten, if indeed they ever knew it. It is a fragile moment. Suddenly a song begins, jolting me out of my reverie. It is a song of which I am very fond, appropriate for the season, but the timing is wrong. Rather than "taking me down," as the song requests, it yanks me out of my most private inner world, leaving me feeling violated. The process is not completed in any effective way, and I feel frightened of being left in the underworld, just as I was approaching an image I since have forgotten.

This has happened before with delicately induced trance states in other rituals, I recall. I feel strongly about attention to timing, with people in such vulnerable states. My background as a therapist makes me aware that this sort of interruption can be more than annoying; it can be dangerous, leaving people unable to integrate the material that has been elicited. In our rush toward egalitarianism, we too frequently violate the trust of the congregation by allowing people to lead complex psychological processes without adequate knowledge or training. As we learned painfully in the early feminist movement, equality does not mean we all have the same level of skill and expertise in all areas. Unfortunately our rituals sometimes suffer from our unwillingness to admit that. ◉⁄◎

Creation: Calling In the New

We are in the null space between what was and what will be. This is the moment of limitless possibilities, out of which we may weave reality anew, if we dare. What will we dare? People wander off in silence to contemplate and envision the possible future.

When we reassemble, we are instructed to move again into a formation in the shape of the DNA molecule. We form a wand of our clasped hands, this time moving clockwise, the direction in which energy naturally moves in this hemisphere. Again we move from altar to altar, naming what we wish to see restored or brought into being: clean air, the ozone layer, caring, commitment, deep feeling, compassion, patience, perseverance, grounding, peace, safety, health, RAIN! (California had been in a severe drought for several years.) In general, our words are more abstract than in the previous section on disintegration. It is easier to be specific about what already exists that we would like to see gone than it is to be highly specific about things that do not yet exist that we wish to bring into being.

Reflections

The problem that becomes apparent as the participants try to envision a future of their making is that they lack the moral, thealogical vocabulary to translate a nature-centered paradigm into concrete images and actions at the level of larger systems. Refugees from the New Age mouth platitudes about only being able to change themselves, about transformation lying solely within and through each individual. The psychological vocabulary and paradigm cannot adequately explain why things are as they are, or how we might be instrumental in changing them, except within a narrow, personal field, because it is based on an atomized view of the individual psyche as causal, at the center of reality. It claims that the social is a mere reflection of the individual. In its inversion of basic feminist theory, it reduces the political to the merely personal. It cannot give direction because it is morally neutral, patriarchal, and implicitly system-supporting. It does not address the whole systems and institutions that frame, shape, and define individual consciousness.

By reducing rich and complex theological concepts like "evil," "goddess," "grace," and "co-creation" to psychological ones like "projecting our shadow," the "inner feminine," or "creating our own reality," we frame ourselves into an ethic of narcissistic individualism bordering on solipsism. This individualistic language and paradigm gives us no moral, conceptual ground from which to intervene in the world. At its worst it is a sort of cosmic or karmic Calvinism in which good fortune proves worthiness, and victimization proves its opposite.

Having forsaken the traditional theological language of salvation, sin, and sacrifice, Neopagans too often find themselves trying to rewrite reality with only visualization and the barrenness of subjectivist psychological vocabulary and paradigm available to them. It is not thealogical ground that is lacking; it is thealogical language. The language and symbol system of organic evolution, which is inherently relational and processive, as well as diverse, needs to fully inform our understanding of our role in large, systemic change.

If we are to find in our rituals a meaning and understanding of our relationships (to the universe and to one another) that guides and liberates, we need a vocabulary of reciprocal relationality and co-creation with the divine. Unless we can claim the authority of the living planet to impact at a whole-systems level;

unless we seek resources, strength, and guidance; unless we understand imaginative visualization to be one part of our sustained actions of co-creation, our visions will remain disincarnate within a patriarchal model of creation in which idea gives birth by word alone, instantly and without the pain of labor. This is far from a feminist, embodied view of creation or change, and far also from nature's way.

It may be time to selectively reclaim traditional theological language. We need to be able to speak of the redemption of Gaia, for example, from those who have her in bondage and are exploiting her unto death. This language shift would redirect consciousness and actions, empowering her advocates as agents of liberation. One might speak of humanity in this time as a people in need of salvation, having become estranged from their Mother Nature. This language has depth and power. It gives direction that is not simply self-absorbed. The resultant magic would automatically become more concrete, and petition more responsible.

How does one get from here to there? People's own lives and work must form the bridge. Just as throwing personal pain or problems into the cauldron is just one step in a larger process of self-transformation, magical envisioning is just one step in the process of social transformation. Envisioning unsupported by action is merely wishful thinking. Such wishful thinking can give rise to a vision of the Goddess as a magic mommy who can and will fix every little thing. I would assert that such a Goddess would not be in the interests of women's liberation and empowerment.

Communion

Now that the ritual has completed its major work, we want just to be with each other. We have new stories, poems, and songs to share, as well as insights and visions from our descent that night. And we are monstrously hungry. It is by now about 4:00 A.M. The potluck food is brought out from the house, blessed, and we sit comfortably in the circle, eating, drinking, singing, talking, and listening.

Reflections

This is a remarkable event, this informal sharing in sacred circle. One of the greatest attributes of Neopagan thealogy and practice is that it does not separate the sacred from the secular. It does not cast outside the circle aspects of life not deemed sufficiently holy. All of life is sacred. Life is (w)hole-y. The sacred is honored in the ordinary. Human laughter, fellowship, remembrance of Samhains past and friends not present, all are sanctified by their inclusion in the circle.

Affirmation and Raising Energy

After a sufficient time of relaxing and informal sharing, we are ready to complete
our ritual work: weaving a web of protection. A large web made of many cords is
carefully unwrapped in the center of our circle. The presiding member explains to
the group that this web was originally woven exactly one year ago in Peru, in a
Samhain ritual shared by some of our group members with the indigenous medicine people there. After wearing them for several days, hosts and visitors had
woven their cords together into a symbol of the unification of indigenous, earth-
loving people in both the Northern and the Southern Hemispheres. Since then,
knots have been added to the web at various conferences and festivals around the
country.

Each knot in the web stands for a wish or prayer for a better world. Now we are
invited to add our own wishes to the web's power. Each person holds one string.
This time we are weaving protection into its magic, for what has already been a
year of hardship and suffering promises to continue through the winter. Magic
alone does not create reality, but like any form of prayer, it increases or decreases
the odds on certain occurrences. By weaving an umbrella of psychic protection, we
hope to prevent some of the fallout and backlash from landing on us.

What is it, then, that we request protection from and for in this elaborated
benediction? Do we ask for protection from the growing plagues of immune dis-
orders and environmental diseases around us, from the fallout of California's trou-
bled economy, the increasing dangers on the streets to ourselves and our children?
No, most of our prayers continue to reflect a paradigm of psychological individualism. One woman asks to be protected from the fear that interferes with her relationships; another asks for protection from her addiction, a third from her anger.
These do not require divine protection, but inner responsibility. Nor is there
mention of the real and objective causes of fear and anger, or protection from
these. Someone calls for protection of the Goddess's people from the wrath of
right-wing fundamentalists and their god. One feminist petitions for protection of
our right to reproductive choice, being threatened by courts and zealots with
guns. Another speaks to the increase of violent crimes against women, and asks
that she and her sisters be protected. A man responds by asking for protection
from male bashing and blame, as if this were comparable. A mother prays for the
protection of children from all forms of abuse. Someone else puts a protection on
the old-growth redwoods of California's North Coast. And so it goes, until we
complete the circle and everyone has had an opportunity to speak. When all present have had the opportunity to add their prayers, the group visualizes a dome of
protection surrounding it. We hold the web high above our heads and begin circling clockwise, singing, "We are weaving our power, we are weaving our magic,
we are weaving our love."[7] We circle and sing until the spell is strong in energy,
then we ground it in the earth.

Reflections

Alas, the solipsistic worldview referred to earlier in this chapter once again frames many prayers. Some of our newer members ask for protection from themselves, as if to say, if I can protect myself from myself, all else will be fine; only my own thought forms can harm me. (Our more seasoned members have a more fully developed thealogy and vocabulary, and are far less reliant on New Age psychometaphysics for their cosmology.) Women lose ground as the language of feminism and interdependence is replaced by the language of addiction and codependence. In spite of its shortcomings, however, this is a powerful exercise in group prayer and participatory magic.

Completion: Opening the Circle

The light will return soon. We must finish our ritual and return to the upper world. It is time to thank the God and Goddess of the underworld for gracing our circle, time to say goodbye to our honored guests and ancestors, time to turn things back around. A new year is beginning. Whatever was done tonight is done. The year will tell us what our magic wrought.

We thank the spirits of earth, air, fire, and water for helping with our magic, and take down the magic circle between the worlds. "All from air into air, let the misty curtain part/All is ended, all is done, what has been must now be gone!/ What is done by Ancient Art must merry meet and merry part and merry meet again."[8] The circle is open, the ritual is over.

* FEMINIST ANALYSIS *

What have we done here, and what have we accomplished? We have honored the deities, both female and male, and our departed ancestors. We have offered the old and the decaying to the Goddess for breaking down and regeneration. We have retrieved lost parts of ourselves. We have shared food, drink, stories, and laughter. We have sung the songs and prayed the prayers. We have honored and said goodbye to the old year and planted seeds for the new one (but we will not know which ones took root until well past the winter solstice). We have woven a web to surround and protect us. We have worshiped and communed, touched and been touched, reflected on our lives in the framework of community and of the greater whole. What then, if anything, makes this ritual more feminist or life-affirming than a new year's ritual in any other tradition?

In this tradition the most important celebrations are seasonal, commemorating not one-time events, but the community's place in the spiral of time/space that is ever turning, and the phases ever repeating themselves within that spiral. By focusing worship on seasonal cycles rather than on historical events, Neopagan celebration locates divinity primarily within nature's processes and cycles, as opposed to a force intervening in human history. It celebrates the human place in nature, rather than placing humans and their god(s) outside of, or above, nature.

This creates problems for some feminists who, in reifying nature, have internalized a nature/culture polarity. They have gone on to identify nature as the source of woman's subordination, and culture as her liberator. Neopagans see the subordination and proprietorship of woman and of nature by the patriarchy as going hand in hand. Nature-centered thealogy does not identify or romanticize woman as being in any way "closer to nature" than man in her basic make-up or essence.[9]

There are, however, several ways in which the Neopagan ritual style and tradition are deeply feminist and empowering to women. The basic equality of female and male is explicit and built in at ground level, as shown by the equal roles of priestess and priest, and the invocations of Goddess and God. Women carry a strong liturgical role, as priestesses of the Goddess. This should not be underrated in its importance. Being able to see oneself and one's religious leaders as a reflection and embodiment of the divine is of inestimable value to women's self-image. It is very different in its impact from a theology of having a neuter soul in a body of "otherness." The deity is embodied, hence all bodies are divine in all their phases and forms. In this case, there is a strongly feminist affirmation of the Goddess embodied in aging women, not just in nubile maidens or nurturers. The gray-haired priestess of our Halloween circle; a strong, active, independent person, is a woman for herself and (w)hole-y. Our Goddess is powerful in all of her changes.[10]

This sets up a relationship to female sexuality and to sexual union as sacred. These principles are fundamental to Goddess worship, and to my mind override the criticisms, contradictions, and complaints I have expressed earlier. Still, contradictions do exist and sometimes even flourish in an atmosphere in which one easily becomes deaf to the subtleties of sexism in language and practice. These are more quickly noticed by vigilant feminists in a more traditionally patriarchal environment, such as the Roman Catholic Church. Sexism can slip by in Pagan groups. And there are other "isms" that grow in an all too often self-congratulatory atmosphere.

Let us take, for example, the location of the retreat center. It is important to nature lovers to celebrate in as wild and private a place as possible, especially for the highest holidays. The church is fortunate to have inherited a fifty-five-acre land trust in the hills of Mendocino, a few hours' drive from San Francisco, where folks can meet, frolic, and worship undisturbed among the trees and deer. This group has occupied, loved, planted, and circled on this land since it became theirs in the mid-1970s. They are, after all, nature worshipers.

The site, however, raises certain problems. It is remote, difficult to reach without four-wheel drive, much less with a wheelchair. It would be extremely difficult for a person with physical disabilities to negotiate its rugged terrain. Its primitive facilities can only support a limited number of members and guests without taxing the land, which the organization is committed to healing. These factors means the church cannot be as inclusive as some members might like it to be, which becomes more of a problem as the group grows.

The number and kind of people who can attend any land-based celebration is always limited, and the question of how to determine who those will be is always a difficult one. Of course it is not only the land that limits numbers. There is also the concern about the quality of participation and how a sense of closeness and safety will be possible if the group is allowed to become too large.

These same questions plagued the early women's consciousness-raising movement: How does a group maintain intimacy, integrity, and safety while building a broad-based, inclusive movement? How does it stand for equality while maintaining an "in-group" of initiates and an "out-group" of newcomers? Conversely, how can it maintain its core values if newcomers have an equal voice in important ideological and policy matters?

This group attempted some of the same solutions as did the women's groups: it created spin-offs. They held open rituals in accessible locations in town on the prior weekend. Attendance at the closed ritual depends on membership, length of involvement, depth of commitment, and promptness of registration. People try to be fair, but for the most part, it is a core group of initiates, those who have been around for years, who are permitted to enter the "holy of holies," the sacred land, at this most sacred time of year. This creates another, even more disturbing problem: those who have been around for years are all able-bodied Caucasian heterosexuals and bisexuals. As both cause and effect of this, the prevailing symbol system and mythology are predominantly heterosexual, the deities predominantly European. Of course, it is theoretically possible for a literate person of any race or sexual preference to move progressively through the church hierarchy into the "in group," and that does happen occasionally, but as the church has no affirmative action program, it is likely to remain largely homogeneous.

Another problem is that as the group expands to let new people into the inner circle, a subtly New Age antihistorical, antifeminist (so-called postfeminist) bias has crept in, couching itself in therapeutic jargon and the language of the men's movement, advocating "men's liberation," which, translated, usually portends a self-justifying refusal to deal with feminist issues or critique.[11] How can a group maintain or stand for a set of values if it is not willing to convert or educate new members?

One of the limitations of a highly participatory ritual style is that, because there is no sermonic form, there is no prophetic voice within the liturgy. There is no place within a worship context for leadership to call members to accountability for racism, sexism, hypocrisy, or the just plain pettiness to which all churches, including this one, seem to fall prey. Should anyone try to do so, they will likely be accused of some New Age faux pas: being anti-male, judging, laying a guilt trip, or, Goddess forbid, preaching. Thus the group's laissez-faire liberalism disarms an implicitly feminist moral imperative by not allowing it to be made explicit in sacred space. The voice of clergy is confined to the priestly and pastoral modes. Without a scripture and a prophetic voice calling the group to integrity within its thealogy, it is easy to fall into mushy moral relativism, and for diversity to devolve into militant individualism.

The question of children's attendance at rituals must also be broached. Arguments have gone on for years about whether to include children in church rituals. Reasons given for their exclusion include their being a distraction (especially to their parents), legal concerns about the sexually explicit symbol system, and the oftentimes late hour of celebrations. Pagan anti-child bias might also be attributed to the tradition of secrecy in its Wiccan roots. One is certainly hesitant to pass on to children an outlaw form of worship, however innocent it may be in reality. Lives have been lost for less.

Ironically, the tendency to exclude children from worship may also be traceable to the group's feminist roots and women's need to experience themselves and their spirituality outside their identities as mothers, lovers, or wives. Many women are still trying to heal themselves spiritually and emotionally from the wounds of their own childhood, and too often there seems to be no emotional room in this for their children. It would be nearly impossible to participate in shamanic trance work, for example, with a small child pulling at one's sleeve. It is true that women need sacred space apart from children.

But what, then, becomes of the children? How do values and traditions get passed to the next generation? How does a genuine worshiping community form itself, as distinct from a healing circle, a coven, or a therapy group? In spite of my not being a mother, or perhaps because of it, I hold children's religious education and their inclusion in most community events to be a primary responsibility of the community. In some ways this community does rather well. The men in this community do better than most when it comes to taking equal responsibility for child care. There are several single fathers among the members. But the community does not take its responsibilities to the next generation seriously enough, as a religious community. This may be because the Neopagan movement is only beginning to awaken to its values and practices as a religion to be passed on, rather than merely a personal pastime or spiritual path to be enjoyed as an adult leisure activity. It may also be that many members from the "me generation" have taken on the rampant narcissism of the dominant society. Busy "spending their children's inheritance," spiritually speaking, perhaps they simply don't want to be bothered.

Finally, and in keeping with the concern stated about the absence of a morally responsible, prophetic voice, there is a subcultural reluctance to assert anything, require anything, or promote anything that could be taken to limit anyone's free choice or be seen as proselytizing. This leaves the community and its children without a clear sense of its moral authority or purpose. As Robert Bellah pointedly asks, if the sacredness of the individual self is all that is shared, where will moral authority come from? As Bellah further points out, one cannot practice citizenship without claiming moral authority.[12] This reluctance, I would assert, is the most serious problem with this new religious movement and its education of the next generation. If the institution is unwilling to recognize itself as an institution and to claim the moral authority to educate its children respectfully in its values, the group has little reason for existence beyond self-service.

As with so many of the issues facing this and other similar groups, having let go of certain oppressive models by which churches have structured themselves and functioned in the past, there is a need to develop new forms. Having abandoned the forms and values that forced women into the roles of caretaker, mother, and educator, the organization has not, at the time of this writing, figured out the best way to take up the slack of religious education by women for children. For starters, a regular women's circle could be held, during which the men would take responsibility for child care. Perhaps it could be reciprocal, with women doing child care for a regularly scheduled men's circle at which no children below the age of puberty are present. But it is vital that teens be present at these same-sex circles, if they are to have the help and role models they need for dealing with the complexities and mysteries of their developing sexuality in loving, safe, and nonsexist ways. It is equally vital, if children are to become responsible adults and community members, that the community as a whole take responsibility for their well-being and religious education, welcoming their presence and modeling active participation at community worship events.

With all the above concerns raised, however, I believe that the single most important thing about this ritual from a feminist perspective, and the thing that distinguishes it from any patriarchal liturgy, is its thealogical purpose. The group is ritualizing and honoring the difficult and troublesome entry into the dark time of year and with it, into the dark parts of themselves. It calls on its honored dead to guide its passage. This custom is as old as human culture. It is fundamental to feminist thealogy and ritual to honor darkness and death, alongside light and birth, as intrinsic to the regenerative process,[13] as we shall more fully see in the next chapter, on the winter solstice.

One is left with the ancient familiarity of this ritual and its humanity. It truly reflects the group as they are and as they hope to be, in all their human frailty and beauty. This is a tradition that has room for the people in it. Perhaps that is because it is still fresh, in the bloom of its youth, not yet having been codified into doctrine. Perhaps the early Christians told stories and laughed, too, as they broke bread in communion. I am certain that pre-Christian people in caves and round-houses around the Mediterranean and in Northern Europe did so. My bones remember this.

OUT OF THE DARKNESS

✳

The Winter Solstice

The summer sun warms my shoulders as I approach the chapter on the winter solstice. I have been avoiding this chapter, putting it off just as I always try to put off the arrival of winter itself. What is it about darkness that makes one want to say, like a child being called in from play or sent to bed, "Oh, please, just five more minutes"? But death and darkness do not wait.

Light is life for all oxygen-based life forms. Human beings, like plants, grow toward the light. Perhaps that is the reason we seek to put off entering darkness until the last. Yet it is from darkness life comes and to darkness that all life returns. Both light and dark are essential parts of earth's life cycle, and although life craves the light, it requires the darkness. Plants and animals burn up or go crazy without sufficient amounts of it.

Darkness and death descend annually upon the world. Every spring the year is reborn. This is simple and unchanging. Although the human impulse is to cling to the last of the light and warmth, as the last leaf clings to the branch, there is wisdom in honoring and learning from the mystery of nature's cycles. Why is there so much avoidance of the simple truths of death and darkness? Must we deny what we cannot control?

One task of ritual is to assist people in their efforts to make peace with the more difficult and painful facts of life, like death and darkness. The central bio-thealogical message in the wheel of the year is this: life and renewal are rooted in darkness and death. At every level of life, from trees shedding their leaves, which form rich mulch for the earth's renewal, to personal spiritual development, in which one lets go of the old to make room for the new, death precedes rebirth. There are vital repair and assimilation functions that bodies can only perform in the dark. During sleep, bodies cleanse and repair cells damaged in the process of living. It is in winter, when shorn of its leaves, that a tree sends roots deeper into the earth, pulling up vital nutrients to restore itself and grow. Without death there is no rebirth. There is only burnout. The well-being of human souls and of their native planet demands that civilization come to terms with these facts of life.

The winter solstice is the shortest day of the year. One can only imagine what it was like before artificial lighting and heat, to see the days becoming shorter and the nights longer. How far might this encroaching darkness go? At what point would the trend reverse? The sun returned last year, but suppose it doesn't this year? Although the solstice marks the beginning of winter in our current calendar, it also marks the turning of the year, when the days begin once again to lengthen. People kept track by following the stars. They held vigil through the longest night to assure the sun's return. In Britain's Newgrange there is a chamber among the standing stones placed thousands of years ago. It allows a single shaft of light in only at dawn only on the morning of the winter solstice: "The rising sun pours into the passageway illuminating for a brief moment the triple spiral carved on the wall of the inner chamber of the earthen burial mound."[1]

We cannot know what use and meaning such a construction had for the people who built it, but we can be sure that it was important to them to know and mark the solstice and the light's returning rays. On this night people gathered in huts and on hillsides, in caves and around fires to watch, to keep faith, and no doubt to tell stories while they waited. These customs gave rise to all the winter festivals of light. Advent's candles lead to the glorious Christmas celebrations of light (or Yule, marking the birth of the Son). In the Roman calendar this same date marked the celebration of the birth of the emperor-god Caesar Augustus. Hanukkah, the Jewish festival of lights, celebrates the continuous burning of the oil lamp in the temple, keeping light and hope alive beyond reason. The new African American holiday Kwanzaa also celebrates light at this darkest time of year. In the moment of greatest darkness, people the world over celebrate the birth of the sun, by one spelling or another.

In dark times people have a need to be reminded that the darkness will not last forever, that while death is necessary for renewal and transformation, new birth will emerge from it. Neopagan celebrations honor the transformative power inherent in the dark mysteries, rather than attempting to obscure them. Pagans do not light a candle against the darkness. They light a candle as an expression of faith in nature's process of death and renewal. They trust that contained inside winter's velvet depths lie the seeds of transformation.

✳ RITUAL DESCRIPTION ✳

The winter solstice is simple. It is waiting. Whatever seeds dropped from the trees to lie dormant through the snow and rain fell long ago in the fall. They are underground, waiting. Whatever new seeds will be planted must wait until spring thaw. There is nothing much to do now, except light a fire and tell stories. It is the year's liminal moment, when the earth is poised between what was and what will be. In that moment of greatest darkness, the light begins its ascent.

It is the waiting in emptiness that wants ritualizing. This does not call for anything elaborate. Winter rituals work best when they are warm and homey. The following describes a simple ritual that I conducted at the Unitarian Fellowship in Porterville, California, a small fellowship consisting of about thirty middle-aged to elderly white and a few Hispanic women and men. For most people attending, it was a first experience of this kind of ritual, performed in circle, with the calling of directions, etc. Therefore I was attentive to the rite's accessibility and "user-friendliness." I wished to give the congregation an understanding of the theology/thealogy of deity immanent in the rhythms and cycles of nature and an opportunity for direct participation in them. This ritual and symbol system, drawing inspiration from our own bodies and a natural world all people share, is easily accessible and inherently familiar, even when it is new to people. When it works well, people should have a sense of coming home to what they had always known but perhaps had temporarily forgotten or misplaced in the web of complex metaphysics woven by more "civilized" religions.

Gathering and First Words

When people arrived, the chairs were arranged in a circle, with a simple altar in the center. On the altar was a white cloth, a goblet filled with water, a rattle, thirty candles arranged in a tray of sand, an uncut loaf of dark bread, and a collection basket. The service began with the fellowship's moderator introducing me to the group as the intern minister at the nearby First Unitarian Church of Fresno. I then introduced Rick, my partner, and thanked them for inviting me. Before formally beginning, I spoke briefly on the meaning and history of solstice celebrations, telling how for thousands of years, people all over Europe and North America built fires on the hillsides to honor the darkness and to call the light to return.

Creating Sacred Space and Presence

"They gathered in circles as we do today, to honor and celebrate the circle of the sun in its circle of the year," I concluded, segueing into the circle casting. Rick then began to beat out the rhythm for "We Are a Circle" on his dumbek. While Rick sang the verses, the congregation sang the repeated chorus, "We are a circle within a circle, with no beginning and never ending." I use this song frequently for circle castings. It has rhythmic movement, while being simple, so people learn it easily and enjoy singing it. The verses call on the four elements of air, fire, water, and earth, in simple, evocative language, which everyone can understand. For example, "Within our blood, within our tears, there lies the altar of living water" reminds the singers that the sacred elements of which life is made also make up their own bodies. "Within our heart there glows a spark, love and desire, a burning fire" asserts that the spark of love is sacred.[2]

This is the death of the year. It is the white, wintry Lady who presides over sleeping, gestating life. She is the one who takes all life into her bosom when it is tired. I invoked the Goddess in her crone personage:

Hail to Thee who dares to see, Who draws the knife and severs life,
And takes away Her children to Her wintry, dark home.[3]

I did not invoke her consort, the God, at the beginning of the ritual, as would be the usual procedure in most seasonal rites. Between Samhain and the winter solstice, Celtic tradition does not call on him. He is dormant, sleeping, waiting to be reborn. The winter solstice celebrates his rebirth as the sun. In the first half of this ritual I wanted the congregation to feel his absence. Later I would use a specific invocation of the sun as God to call him forth.

✳ EXPOSITION: CREATING A CENTRAL SYMBOL ✳

The central symbol in this winter rite was neither darkness nor light, but the relationship between the two as interdependent parts of a whole, or moving points on a dynamic continuum. Just as the year goes from darkness to light, this ritual follows the same pattern of invoking darkness, then moving toward light. We would need to reframe the darkness for people, as a place that need not be frightening.

Many people associate darkness with something evil or sinister. When Neopagans say they enter the darkness they do not refer to anything demonic or inverted; they refer to the place where old, worn-out forms break down in decay, making rich compost for the fertile womb of earth to renew life. They refer to the restful darkness in which the inchoate gestates until it is ready to take form. To enter the darkness, which we believe to be the only way to transformation and rebirth, is our act of supreme faith in the regenerative power of our Goddess.

Good and evil are independent of darkness and light, and can occur with an excess of either. Lucifer, after all, is known as the light bearer. A nuclear bomb has the light of a thousand suns. Light is not "good." Neither is darkness "bad." This association has not only racist but sexist overtones. It was this association with darkness that I aimed to debunk in my homily, by creating positive associations to darkness in its power to gestate the earliest stages of new life. My central point was that all life begins in the darkness—animal life in the darkness of an egg or in the womb of its mother, plant life in the darkness of the earth, underground, hidden from our eyes. The homily evoked the deep, dark processes of gestation: of biological life, and of ideas. There is a time to leave things alone, to let them gestate in their inchoate state until they are sufficiently strong to survive exposure. A seedling takes root in the damp, dark earth before sending up shoots toward the sun. A human fetus develops for nine months in the protective darkness of its mother's womb before coming out into the light. Premature exposure kills. Winter is the gestating, waiting time for earth creatures.

I followed my talk with a song by songwriter Frankie Armstrong, who has a special relationship to the darkness, being a woman of severely limited sight. She wrote this song for the women who kept year-round vigil at Greenham Common in protest of the British deployment of the American cruise nuclear missiles.

Out of the darkness comes the fear of what's to come.
Out of the darkness comes the dread of what's undone.
Out of the darkness comes the hope that we can run,
And out of the darkness comes the knowledge of the sun.

Darkness is a place of birth, darkness is the womb,
Darkness is a place of rest, darkness is the tomb,
Death belongs to life, half of day is night,
[We need not fear the darkness], but the blinding flash of light.

Out of the darkness comes the fear of the unknown,
Out of the darkness comes the dread of bleaching bone,
Out of the darkness comes the hope we're not alone,
And out of the darkness grow the seeds that we have sown.[4]

Reflections

The autumn equinox and Halloween lead irrevocably to the darkness of solstice. Darkness and liminality form the empty core of this seasonal moment, before the fulcrum swings back in the other direction. We stop. We wait in the dark. We cannot force or hurry or control the outcome. We honor the waiting. The entire opening section of this ritual is oriented toward accepting and honoring what is, trusting the Goddess to determine what will be.

Purgation

This was a simple ritual. It called for a simple emptying out, more contemplative than purgative. A few moments of silent meditation, accompanied by dulcimer music, were all that was needed. People were invited to consider what was decomposing and what taking root in the darkness of their own lives. We followed this by passing the rattle around the circle and allowing people to share, Quaker meeting style, their impressions from the meditation. They had the option of remaining silent and simply holding the rattle before passing it on.

Reflections

Every ritual has a turning point. The contemplative moment was the turning point of this ritual. Because winter is a time of dormancy, the turning of this rite is one of contemplation rather than of action. In the silence, people absorb the sense of emptiness, of no-thing. Purgation happened in the fall, when leaves fell from the tree and people placed their extra baggage into the cauldron. Now one waits in emptiness. All that we must continue to purge ourselves of is our desire to control or hurry the outcome.

Calling In the New

In the next ritual action of lighting candles in silence, the congregation declared its faith in the future and in the returning light that arises from this darkness. There were thirty candles arranged on the center altar, one for each person. I lit the first, explaining that while our ancestors honored the darkness, they also lit fires, symbol of the returning sun, to keep warmth and hope alive through the winter months. "So we, too, light a candle to hope for what will arises from the dark earth in the spring of our year," I said. I invited the members of the congregation to silently light their own candles in hope and in faith for what cannot yet be seen or named. One at a time they came forward and did so.

Following the meditation the congregation affirmed their faith by singing a traditional winter song that paraphrases the famous fourteenth-century mystic Julian of Norwich, who affirmed, "All shall be well, . . . all manner of things shall be well again."

Reflections

In the lull between light and dark, in the darkest time of the year, there is no invocation of the new, no planting of seeds. An affirmation of faith and hope is more appropriate. This faith is grounded in the benevolence of the universe itself, rather than something that will save the elect from its processes and transformations. Hope lies not in God's transcendent constancy, but in deity immanent within transformation. This value is consistent with a woman-oriented way of worship, as Northup points out in her study of diverse women's rites: "The one theme that seems to arise most consistently [in women's ritualizing] is that whatever the numinous is, it is immanent rather than transcendent."[5]

Affirmation by Communion

In a ritual whose purpose is to affirm faith in the darkness, what better affirmational action is there than a simple communion of bread and water? I used a blessing that reiterated the theme of death giving birth to life, this time using the rain as the image, appropriate to the California winter where, except in the mountains, there is much rain and little or no snow.

BLESSING OF THE WATER

Ice in the north will melt into the Earth.
The Earth will soften and breathe again.
Water, sweetened by the lungs of the Earth
Runs south to the houses of the people.
The clouds give birth and die.
They tremble on beds of air giving birth.
Their trembling rocks the Earth with thunder.
All their life is gone; their last breath is in our cup.
Let us drink the rain.[6]

The simple life-sustaining act of drinking water is thus sanctified, that we not take it for granted. Water is indeed blood of the earth processed by the biosphere in clouds. Lesley Northup points out that women's rituals often celebrate simple domestic acts that identify the sacred with the everyday and with the natural world.[7] The blessing above provides an example of this phenomenon, extending this apparently female sensibility into a mixed worship setting. "Blessing of the Bread," by the same author, calls bread "Rocks of Sun for the tables of humanity," from the marriage of sun and earth, merged in the seed that falls on the "wet spring table."[8]

Simultaneous with passing the basket of bread around the circle for each person to take and eat, the collection basket is passed, so that we may give as we have partaken. Rick plays a reprise of "Bells of Norwich" quietly in the background as people give and receive in the ebb and flow of life.

The service concludes its celebration of light and darkness, rebirth and death, giving and receiving. Miraculously, in the moment of greatest darkness, the light begins its return, once again lengthening our days. So at the end of our service, we have arrived at the beginning, the time to call forth the Sun God. The ritual concludes with the following invocation to the sun as God, adapted from an ancient Egyptian prayer by the Pharoah Akhenaton.

HYMN TO THE SUN

Oh Sun: Creator and source of all terrestrial life . . .
We developed eyes to witness your bounteous light.
Fish leap out of the water into you
And crawled out onto the land to follow your gaze.
So does the lizard love to bathe in your light;
You are his mobility.

Earth life greets You rising in the East and calls after You as You disappear;
Roosters crow and cows moo with the coming and going of Your great light.

Birds fly to the treetops to sing their evening songs in Your last rays.
They follow You as our Mother Earth tips Her face North and South.
Bees always look at You and fly toward You.

Sunflowers, Morning Glorys, all green leaves turn toward You as the Source.
The whole Planet yearns to be One with You through Her creatures.

Let a new Golden Age begin for all Your children.
May You reign forever!
We love You with Your own Love, O our God Star.[9]

There is a chant affirming "We turn toward the light through the darkest night."[10] The service concludes with a brief benediction, thanking and blessing the people and the elements that attended our rites.

Reflections

That which began in darkness has ended in a glorious praising of the sun as source of all life. The invocations of Goddess, early in the ritual, and of God, at the end, reflected the common, perhaps stereotypical associations of female with the dark and male with the light. However, the ritual reframed and reclaimed the darkness as a source of transformation, while affirming the need for a balance of dark and light in the creation and sustenance of life. Both are stages on the ever-turning wheel of the year. Neither is more important than the other, or more worthy of honor.

✳ FEMINIST ANALYSIS ✳

Women's bodies echo the lesson of nature surrounding us: all life comes out of the darkness. To say otherwise is to perpetuate patriarchy's most fundamental deceit: that the male principle alone creates life. I would assert that the reintroduction of darkness as a sacred symbol of creation is essential to a feminist cosmology, because woman creates life in the darkness of her womb.

Darkness did not always carry such negative associations. Archeologist Marija Gimbutas tells us that in the gynocentric religion of Paleolithic and Neolithic Europe, black was the color of fertility, like the earth, while the white of bleaching bones signified death. In Chinese culture white still is the color of death, and black, of life. It was at the time of the Indo-European invasions during the fifth and sixth millennia B.C.E. that (male) deity began to be identified almost entirely with light. At that point artifacts representing deity show a startling transition from predominantly female-embodied images to male warriors holding thunderbolts.[11] This was the beginning of the worship of the God of light who claims to create by word, or idea, alone. Simultaneous with the subordination of the Goddess, women, and the body was the systematic profanation of all the fleshy processes that happen in the dark.[12]

During the ascent of patriarchy, the mythology of creation eventually arrived at a tale in which a male god made woman from a man's rib, with no darkness or gestation involved. The denial of darkness goes hand in hand with the denial of birth by woman and the suppression of physicality. We find such blatant denial in Aeschylus' tale of the *Eumenides,* in which Athena defends the patriarchy and father-right by her assertion that a father can give birth unaided, offering as evidence her own origin from Zeus's head.[13]

Hand in hand with the degradation and denial of the body goes the diminution of the earth, of matter, and of mater, all attributed to the "feminine." The physicality of creation is replaced with a sanitized metaphysic, which denies sex, death, motherhood, and decay—all the messy processes that shake the human pretense to invincibility. If creation is conceived as purely metaphysical, through spirit alone, we may pretend that we are safe from death. We find within this cosmology the grounds for the degradation of the body, and of the supposedly more physical female, as less worthy than the more spiritual male.[14] For example, Aristotle tells us that "while the body is from the female, it is the soul that is from the male, for the soul is the reality of a particular body."[15] It is not far down the slippery slope from this thinking to the *Malleus Maleficarum,* the lengthy medieval Dominican text and apologia for witch burning, which, in equating evil and the body, asserts that women are prey for the devil by virtue of their inherent carnality: "But the natural reason is that she is more carnal than a man, as is clear from her many carnal abominations. And it should be noted that there was a defect in the formation, since she was formed from a bent rib, that is a rib of the breast, which is bent in a contrary direction to a man. And since through this defect she is an imperfect animal, she always deceives."[16]

If feminists are to redeem bodies and sexuality from the gods of light, they will also have to redeem the darkness from the racist and sexist associations that have been made since it became dissociated from its natural, seasonal realm. Such redemption ought to become a central feature of feminist winter rites marking the passage from darkness to light.

A LITTLE BIT OF LIGHT

*

Candlemas

Even in Northern California, there are times when it seems it will never be spring. This year has been dark and damp since Halloween. Everyone is cranky after the holidays, and try though one might to bootstrap motivation with New Year's resolutions, no one can seem to pick up much momentum.

This is the dark time, when life grows underground with no external proof of its existence. Demanding proof could kill it. Leave the roots alone, they are germinating. Seeds are breaking through their shells and sending out fragile feelers into the cool, moist earth, looking for something to grab onto. There is nothing to sustain one now but faith, the evidence of things not seen, and a fundamental trust in nature's regenerative powers. Life feels cold and unsure. People turn inward, like young seedlings groping in the inchoate darkness for they know not what.

Then one day very early in February, just between the winter solstice and the spring equinox, something begins to stir gently. Who knows what it is? Life. Perhaps an early calla lily or daffodil, the first pussy willows. Perhaps it is internal, a stirring in one's own body. A sense of restlessness, or even irritability, takes over. Something is coming, but no one is sure of what. Suddenly the day is—no, not a lot, just a little, but still noticeably longer. The beginning of the end of winter, the early rumors of spring, are almost palpable, like a seed planted deep in the belly which one can only sense, but not yet feel.

This is the day the ancient Celts called Imbolc, when they honored the pregnant solar goddess of the forge known as Brigde. It is called the Feast of Brigde, or Brigit, Candlemas, and Groundhog's Day. People in all northern traditions celebrate the returning light and the quickening seed. Almost automatically one begins to sweep out the winter doldrums. Get out the broom, and make sure that all the solstice decorations are down and put away. It is considered bad luck to have them still out when Brigde comes. It is time to make room for the new, for the spring, for planting and flowers, and the seeds that will become this year's vegetables. Light is returning, and all hasten to make ready the place it will enter. Irish country folk swept and cooked and made their cottages ready for the visiting pregnant goddess dressed as a bride with the seed of spring in her womb.[1] All this because human bodies and the earth respond to the little bit of light on the horizon.

❋ RITUAL DESCRIPTION ❋

The following ritual was offered for the celebration of Candlemas in 1992. It took place at the Sufi house in San Rafael, California, presented by a group called Spirit Live, which produced monthly participatory, inspirational events. Because it was a Sunday-morning event, for a group seeking a modified Sunday worship experience, the design group wanted it to fit into a more or less familiar worship format, incorporating ritual elements in a conventional Western liturgical style. We had an hour and a half, a small group of performers and musicians willing to experiment, and a congregation of about fifty participants.

Our intention was for people to come out of the service affirming the light that was returning to their lives, however scant it might be, and able to embrace what it revealed. The primary message of the service was that what at first appears ugly and makes people want to turn away is often the beginning of transformation and growth. February is not necessarily a pretty time of year. In the northern regions, the snow that has covered things all winter turns to sludge and ice. Everyone is tired of winter. There seems to be a layer of dust on everything. Seeing with that bit of returning light is the call to begin cleaning to make room for spring planting—whether in one's back yard or one's heart. This is the lesson of Candlemas, a faith lesson. How can one make ready for the unknown, with no evidence of its coming?

The group begins to paint the community ritual with a wash, as in a watercolor. What is the background color or mood of the community? It is their story that the service tells, and, in the telling, transforms. In the weeks before the service, I interviewed people in the group on what they were noticing, feeling, and thinking about in their own lives and in the larger world. I listened to conversations in restaurants and coffee shops, gleaning a sense of the common note being struck by the world and by the community.

I discovered I was not alone in having a severe case of winter doldrums that year. Californians were worried. They felt shrouded, buried by darkness. Nothing seemed to be moving or growing. California was in a severe drought. The state economy had hit a serious low. There had recently been massive layoffs and downsizings in the high-tech industries that support much of the state. This was not what people had expected a few short years ago in the affluent eighties, when many people had gone into business for themselves or taken on higher costs of living. Now people were concerned about keeping their homes and feeding their families.

The artists and entrepreneurs who made up a significant portion of the community we served were wondering if they would make it. Seeing a daily increase in homelessness on the streets, many community members were all too aware that they were a mere paycheck or two, or a client or two, away from adding to its numbers. The ambient mood was gray. How, in this atmosphere, could we create a service that was inspirational, that would encourage people to affirm the light in their lives even as it illumines what they do not wish to see? Ritual must begin from where the people are. No sacred space is possible that is not grounded in acknowledging the lived truth of people's lives and which does not address their concerns and suffering. Especially at this time of sweeping out the winter doldrums, people must be willing to name them and claim them. They are our own, and we can only transform what we call our own.

This was not an easy sell in this New Age group. Some members of the creative team, who wanted the service to be inspiring, believed in positive thinking. They did not see how speaking pain or anger could provide hope and inspiration. They did not wish to "dwell on the negative," to "give it power," as they put it. But inspiration built on a foundation of undisclosed fear and worry, despair and shame, is not inspiration at all, but denial disguising itself as hope. There is no power for transformation in denial. The question is not how to ignore our pain and suffering in the name of transcendence, but how to affirm life and truth in the face of pain and suffering.

Gathering, Purgation, and Creating Sacred Space

The color of the ritual atmosphere was gray, like the season, with soft yellow poking through like the bit of sunlight we anticipate. We used these colors in the invitations and announcements, as well as on the altar, arranged with a soft gray cloth and laid with pussy willows, daffodils, and white candles. The chairs were arranged in a modified circle with the pulpit and singers making up about a third of the perimeter, the congregation making up the other two-thirds, in concentric, loose rows. There was what might be called a playing area in the center, where the dance, performance, and ritual elements (such as the candle ceremony) would take place.

The service began with humor, taking people off guard. This service, more than most, plays on the juxtaposition of the familiar and the surprising. People do not expect a worship or inspirational event to be humorous or irreverent. But one of the principles behind the grouping of liturgists and performers who make up the creative team is to push the boundaries of ritual and theater, to use performance to heal and transform in a participatory setting.

I called upon one person to speak the outrageous for us all: the anger, the frustration, the despair, even what we normally do not allow ourselves to air aloud, especially in public. Olivia Corson is a performance artist and monologist who speaks honestly what most of us only think about the contradictions of modern life and our own humanity. She is an ecofeminist. She has humor and compassion. She could get us laughing at ourselves and at the absurdity of our world. She was perfect for the job.

She entered after the ushers had seated the congregation and the pianist was concluding a lush, meditative prelude. All seemed to be serenely spiritual. Olivia's harried entrance jarred us out of our Sunday-morning reverie. Is there no peace? She thrusts her baby into her husband's surprised arms. "Here. You hold her," she demands. Then, gesticulating wildly, she begins to talk about how life is for her— how she reaches the edge of her coping ability trying to juggle economic and creative needs and still remain a good citizen and mother, negotiating lines at the Safeway while grants are drying up and the baby is peeing on her.

I do not want people to be sure at first that Olivia is performing. Perhaps she is just the harried mother of a small child gone slightly over the edge trying to make ends meet, as she points to our attempts to keep it all together inside the insanity of our daily lives. We laugh, uncomfortably at first, then warmly. She is the crazy woman inside us all. We recognize our stressed-out selves in our February irritability with the gray weather and our concerns about how to just get through without killing someone. By bringing our feelings out in the open instead of stepping over them, her monologue has helped us begin the process of bringing our lives to the light. We have set up a question, a dilemma for the service to address: where is the hope, the light, the holy, in all this fragmentation, frustration, and worry? Where lies redemption? Where is a little bit of light?

People are invited to voice their complaints and frustrations aloud, all at once. After a moment, over the babble of voices, a chant begins in the eastern corner of the room, quietly at first, then catching hold and rising from the congregation in four parts, filling the room with a round of voices.

I know this rose will open.
I know my fear will burn away.
I know my soul will unfurl its wings.
I know this rose will open.[2]

Reflections

The telling of this community's story has begun. It has begun with a reflection of our fragmented and edgy lives. Always in life there is the juxtaposition of everydayness, dirty diapers, hurried meetings, deadlines, people to feed, bills to pay, with moments, if one is attentive, of appreciation, insight, and grace. Always we walk a line between being bogged down in the daily tasks and duties that make up our lives, and transcending them into a greater whole. Conventional patriar-chal liturgy has avoided the former in favor of the latter. A look at the traditional Anglican service, for example, finds little about life's dailiness except in the announcements or maybe the dreaded sermon, which often seems an intrusion into the tapestry of elegant formality and timeless music. While we may find this refuge inspiring, it does little to alter the quality of the lives we return to.

I deliberately wished to disturb the formality and calm that white nonevangel-icals usually equate with the presence of God. I insist on calling forth the pres-ence of the divine in the dirty diapers, in the chaos of life's creation and mainte-nance. I wish to re-sacralize the everyday experience of human beings in a con-fusing, fast-paced, often contradictory world. This is one of women's substantive contributions to theology and liturgy: recognition of the sacred in the everyday, celebrating "the worldly rather than the transcendent."[3] We find this impulse in womanist authors from Zora Neale Hurston to Alice Walker, in feminist theorists from Adrienne Rich to Mary Daly. Women know that life's most sacred act, giv-ing birth, is neither peaceful nor neat; why would worship be?

In this act of defying what is usually considered acceptable in worship, we raise a mirror for people to see their own lives and struggles as sacred. How would we live and relate to one another and to our own humanity if we grasped every moment of our days as part of the sacred? Would we have more compas-sion toward one another and toward ourselves? One can only hope so. Certainly the exhortations to compassion against a backdrop of self-righteous piety and order that is completely discontinuous with our lives will not evoke it. Leaving upsets, concerns, and frustrations at the church door only ensures that we will retrieve them when we go home. Perhaps bringing our raggedy lives and tem-pers smack into the middle of a worship setting will bless them and send us forth with a newfound grace, like the ancient mariner who at last found redemption when he blessed the monsters that had been taunting him.

It is worth noting that we first created the comfort and order of traditional worship by having people seated by ushers and a beautiful prelude played. If there is not some marking of the container, some defining of sacred space apart from the everyday, the service has no transformational power. It is by bringing our familiar disorder into the order of what has been articulated as sacred space that the ordinary is recontextualized in a reflective mode. By allowing for the expression of frustration in our sacred space, we say, "This, too, is sacred." We overlay a song not of hope, but of faith in the generative spirit of life to transform everything, to open roses and burn away fear. We assert the power of souls to open and unfurl their wings because that is what souls, left to their own devices, will do. That is why we know this rose will open. Life never remains frozen for long. Although we cannot see it, we know that spring will come.

It is also worth noting that a sacred space has been created by having ushers greet and seat people in a three-quarters circle, with a pulpit in the front and a piano to one side, thereby marking the threshold of the space as "church." A circle has been subtly cast by the singing of a round, which encircles the worshipers in sound. There are different sorts of circles for different occasions. This occasion calls for something more like a huddle than like a crucible of transformation. The ritual is an affirmation of faith. A tight circle or container is not required. The circle can be loose and permeable, but it should be defined. ✺

Invoking

After the song, serving as minister, I led the group in a pastoral prayer, inviting the blessing of the forces of earth, air, fire, and water, and then the force that calls forth seedlings to reach up out of their safe womb of earth toward the light. I asked that spirit to be with us in community. Then we experimented with a form that became a signature of this community for as long as these services were held. We offered a group prayer, in which everyone had the opportunity to voice their own heartfelt prayer, addressing the sacred in whatever way they saw fit. This was not unusual. What was unusual was the addition of music and dance to prayer.

There was a clear space in the center of the circle where a dancer waited in stillness. As people spoke aloud, one by one, directly addressing the divine by whatever name, the dancer and the pianist together translated each prayer into tones and movement. When all who wished to had spoken, the dancer and the pianist offered an improvisation on what had occurred, a group tone and body prayer offered for and from all of us as a community. Then one of the group members read a passage from the Tao on the great Nothingness, the void out of which all comes and to which all returns. This set up the homily.

Reflections

This experimental form moved prayer beyond the spoken word, where it often gets bogged down, to an artistic expression that engaged our other senses. Often liturgists behave as if the spirit that receives prayer only speaks English. I am convinced that it speaks and understands trees blowing in the breeze, a wolf's howl, a baby's cries, drumming, and bodily movement at least as well, particularly when intention is present. It was beautiful and moving to see the people's words of hope and fear translated into music and dance, and lifted up for gods and friends to share. It took our concerns from the realm of the merely personal, placing them in a shared platform. ✺

Homily: Defining a Central Symbol

Humans interpret the lessons of nature through words, words woven into story. It is for this reason that I chose to speak of the season's returning light through the well-known fairy tale *Beauty and the Beast*. The Disney movie had recently been released, so the story was fresh and familiar to most people. And fairy tales, like myths and Bible stories, have archetypal figures that represent powerful human tendencies and urges to which we can all relate. In my homily for Candlemas, I used *Beauty and the Beast* to illustrate how people want to turn from the light when it reveals something they do not wish to see, and to make a point about transformation: Anything, however ugly or frightening, when brought into the light, has the potential for conscious transformation. It was a lesson about faith in the power of transformation, faith in the power of seeing things as they are, and daring to tell the truth about what we see.

I began the sermon by talking about the returning light, and how, at this stage, it is so indistinct that we can't quite tell whether what we see is a new dawn or the light of an oncoming train. I pointed to the mirror image in the earth's cycles, when we can't tell yet which little shoot is a weed and which is something we planted. Referring back to the reading of the Tao, I observed that everything new emerges from that which is nameless. It is slowly revealing itself.

But, I pointed out, often at the first sign of the light that we eagerly awaited, we turn away. What reveals itself is not pretty. What happens when we move the sofa and shine the light on that corner of the room where we haven't swept in years? Or when we begin to shine the light on those parts of ourselves that we have kept hidden? The child who has been locked in a dark closet does not emerge happy and healthy but distorted and terrified, probably in a rage.

That is exactly what happens in the story of *Beauty and the Beast*. Beauty begins her quest by expressing a wish to find something more in life than the day-to-day. This is where many of us begin our spiritual journeys, with a desire to go beyond the surface of life, to a deeper understanding. And what is the first thing our heroine finds? The Beast. Just as you and I have found when we have delved beneath the nice façade of ourselves, our family history, our nation's military and corporate policies. There it is, ready to devour us.

This is not what we had in mind when we went wandering away from the boundaries of our safe worlds. Our first impulse is to run for cover, just as Beauty does. It is the same impulse that many businesses have succumbed to when the truth was revealed about silicon implants or toxic dumping. It is the same impulse the U.S. government followed in covering up radiation experiments on unsuspecting citizens in the 1950s, and which the Soviet government followed in their attempt first to cover and then to minimize the Chernobyl disaster. It is a human impulse to cover it, hide it, put it back in the box. It is intolerable to look upon the face of the Beast. Everything in us wants to look away, run away.

"Oh, it's not so bad."

"Problem, what problem?"

" A little bit of radiation won't hurt you."

"I don't recall that meeting. No one told me anything."

"Daddy never would have done such a thing. You (or I) must have been imagining."

"It's not a real lie, it's just a little white lie."

"We don't want the homeless HERE. Let them go somewhere else."

How come? What is our impulse to deny, deny, deny? What is so awful about just telling the truth? Is it apathy? Are we just out for ourselves and we don't care? Or is it something more? What really is apathy? If we examine the word we see it means *without* feeling, a refusal to feel. But why would we refuse to feel something?[4]

Perhaps we are afraid that we can't take it. "If I let myself think about it I would go crazy." Or, "If I thought about it I couldn't do my job." Or maybe, "It would create a panic in the public."

But why? Why are we all so afraid of that? Why are we afraid of showing the truth even about ourselves to ourselves? Why do we turn from that little bit of light? Why do we think that our friends, families, neighbors, and customers can't take the truth? Why do we think that we can't take it, ourselves? Why do we tell ourselves that it is better—for that is always what we tell ourselves—to lie, lie, lie? WHY?

We seem to be afraid that what we see will remain like that forever. Could it be that we lack trust—in ourselves, our government, our gods, the universe—to be able to alter what we see? Do we think ourselves powerless? If so, we must pretend reality out of existence. If we are very good at it, sometimes we forget that we are pretending. Then we can be very sincere.

As the song says, you can run but you can't hide. Eventually it comes out or traps you in some way. Look at the Watergate tapes. Look at those parts of yourself that have destroyed relationships or careers. Look at addictions.

Beauty tries to run at first, but she becomes trapped in the Beast's castle. There is no place to go. She can't hide, either. Eventually she accepts the Beast, mostly because she has no choice. She acknowledges it as HER Beast. She then does a courageous thing. She invites the Beast into the light. She does the unthinkable. She looks straight at it.

The moment we invite what was hidden into the light, something miraculous and totally natural occurs. It begins to transform. When sunlight shines on that new shoot, the miracle of photosynthesis occurs. As the plant transforms the light into food, it grows strong. When Beauty looks straight at the Beast, without recoiling, the Beast is transformed.

When we shine our light in those dark, creepy places in our lives, transformation occurs. We are no longer hostages of the parts of ourselves or our past we have kept hidden. We have set the prisoner free. By setting it free we set ourselves free from its shameful hold on us. We begin to see the world anew. I think I see a little bit of light.

In the light or in the dark, we see how nature works, breaking things down, growing new things in the remains. Transformation is not only possible, it is inevitable. The universe is transformation. Nothing remains constant. Nothing made by nature is impervious to change. It is changing all the time. We can trust that. We can put our faith in that process by which life creates and re-creates itself. Divine transformation.

And now, as the days begin to lengthen, we can see that the light is coming, with its transforming powers. Will you let it in? Will you trust it? Will you let it shine and transform even those places you would rather not see? (At this point, music starts vamping behind as musicians begin playing "A Little Bit of Light.")

I think I see a little bit of light. It may not be all pretty, but I can trust it. I know that light will lead me to freedom. I know that light is going to transform my life, if I let it in. I'm going to have faith in that light. (The song begins.)

Reflections

Most rituals have a point of turning, a reversal of direction. It could be the movement from past to future, from despair to empowerment, from stating what is now the case to declaring what will be the case, or from emptying out to taking in something new.[5] In this particular piece the homily provided the center, or turning point, of the ritual. I used this form for several reasons.

First, I have always had a fondness for good preaching, and there was a point I wanted to make that I thought could best be made and illustrated cognitively, with words. Using a homily also fit with my intention to put a nature-centered celebration and symbol system inside a more conventional church service form. Finally, I believe the sermon fills a need that is not otherwise addressed in ritual. It reflects on our lives and struggles in a prophetic voice, providing insights and allowing us to see things that we might otherwise miss.

There is always the question of what to use for homiletical text, if one does not rely solely on the usual Greek or Hebrew Scriptures for inspiration and guidance. What is it that the scriptures traditionally provide? I would suggest that they provide a good story with a history and powerful archetypes that people can put themselves inside of, a story open enough to be told from many different perspectives and viewpoints, and thus to make points at many different levels. There is no single point to the story of Job, or to Jesus' teaching parables. There are many points, which may be applied to many human dilemmas, and the preacher can dwell inside the story until the one that fits best presents itself. There is a sort of universality to scripture. We find ourselves reflected in Job's trials, Peter's fear, Mary's grief. For many people, Biblical models impart a sense of certainty and trust.

What else can offer such guidance and certainty, such archetypal universality, such resonance? Only the direct revelations of nature, as a manifestation of the divine itself, can speak so powerfully and gain trust so completely. There is deep wisdom for us in nature's cycles of birthing and dying, light and darkness. But for the most part, people do not glean wisdom directly from nature, especially in a highly verbal, urban world. Few people any longer have the time, the inclination, or the training to go out into the wild and receive a direct message from Hawk or Gray Wolf. In such a world it is easy to forget nature's teachings and the simple, amazing, humbling fact that our bodies and life cycles are part of and mirror a larger set of seasonal transformations. If humans are to begin to live in harmony with the natural world, honoring its wisdom and cycles as our own, it is up to religious leaders to elucidate these lessons. If preachers were to take the nature's miraculous occurrences as direct revelation from the generative life force, Sunday-morning sermons would interpret physics and the wonders of biology as template for reflecting on human dilemmas. Myths and fairy tales, as well as Bible stories, allow for homiletics. Many ancient myths are nature-based. 🌀

Calling In the New

All join in the choruses, while our singers sing the verses of this gospel-style, or what is called contemporary spiritual, song:

A LITTLE BIT OF LIGHT

Verse 1
Once I could hear only your silence,
Haunted by my shadow in your winterland,
Now I know, I know your light is golden
As you sing to me.

Chorus 1
I think I see a little bit of light
Shinin', shinin' down on me,
I think I see a little bit of light
Where the clouds used to be,
And every day the sun comes out and shines a little bit more,

And someday soon, if I hold out, she'll knock upon my door,
I think I see a little bit of light,
Shinin' down, shinin' shinin' down on me.

Chorus 2
I think I see a little ray of hope,
Smilin', smilin' down on me,
I think I see a little ray of hope
Through the rain, across the sea,
And if I look on down the road, it shines past all of my fear,
Tellin' me if I can just hold on, it's gonna shine right here.
I think I see a little ray of hope, shinin' down, shinin' down on me.

Verse 2
When I am alone feeling forsaken,
And my life has fallen into a frozen dream,
Then your warmth and strength will draw me onward,
Thawing like a stream.

Chorus 3
I think I feel a little seed of life,
Pushin', pushin' out through me,
I think I see a little seed of life
Movin' out, breakin' free,
As ice and snow begin to melt inside the frozen ground
That seed of joy comes pushin' out, a miracle unbound.
(Vamp refrain to end:)
Thank you for the freedom, thank you for the freedom, thank you for
    the freedom, to enjoy . . .[6]

Reflections

A ritual constructed in the form of an evangelical church service turns from despair to empowerment through its sermon. It is followed, like the sermons of many African American worship services, by a song that engages the audience in a high-energy musical affirmation of the sermon's main point. The song takes the cognitive and emotional content spoken from the pulpit and allows the congregation to make it their own through kinesthetic and auditory engagement. They affirm that they too see "a little bit of light." Life, with all its blemishes is embraced, not because it is without darkness or beasts, but because we have the power to transform it by our engagement with it. We give thanks for the freedom to enjoy life, just as it is. ❧

Offering

In this ritual the offering is placed right at the pivotal point, after the homily and before the "altar call." People are invited to give generously while the song continues in the background. Ushers pass the baskets. This gives the offering a central role in calling the community as a whole to affirm the faith and gratitude called for in the sermon.

Reflections

The offering is the moment many liturgists dread. Some regard it as a necessary evil and treat it as such. Some ministers would like to take it out of the service altogether, and they may occasionally manage to do that, through pledges paid monthly. Sometimes people place a basket unobtrusively at the entryway, which yields little. The manner in which most ritualists handle it says, "This is not important. We apologize for having to trouble you with money. A few pennies will be fine."

But a few pennies are not enough to support this work. Just the hard costs of the ritual—hall rental, flowers, parking, coffee and tea, candles, communion bread, and whatever else is needed—may take money out of the planners' own pockets, which may not be deep. The group found this to be a big problem in these Spirit Live events. People would put quarters or a dollar into the collection plate, based, I suppose, on what their mothers had handed them to put in the collection plate when they were children. (It interests me that the same people who pay $7.50 for a movie will contribute only $2 or $3 for a ritual. Do they get less value from a ritual? If so, they should go to a movie instead.) When we counted the money, we would find we were short. Often the people who had worked hard all month planning found themselves having to come up with $25 or $50 they could ill afford.

From a feminist perspective, the offering is the individual's and community's support of spiritually transformed reality. This portion of the ritual, then, needs to reflect the intentionality of such an investment in a common vision. Some ritualists simply levy a charge at the door. I prefer not to charge for ritual. Ritual is worship, among other things, and worship should be free to all. How, then, is it possible to cover the real costs of such events? I believe ritualists and ministers must educate their communities to pay willingly for what nourishes their souls.

This means there should be no apologies in the taking of the collection. Worship leaders might take it openly and joyously, as part of the celebration, asking people to give in that same spirit. ◉

Affirmation, Commitment, and Raising Energy

Since we had been talking about shining light in dark places, we invited the members of the congregation to light a candle. As they did so, they named the thing they would shine light on—named it in just a word or two, so as to keep the service flowing. What were they willing to expose to the light of day? What young shoot might need gentle sunlight to grow?

As people came forward, one by one, to light a candle and say their word, the singers and musicians continued to play and hum the theme from "Little Bit of Light," using each person's word as refrain. Pretty soon all joined in, creating a ceremony of community which powerfully reflected back and affirmed what each person chose to name. So as one person lit her candle and said "family," for example, everyone sang, "fa-mi-ly, fa-mi-ly, fa-mi-ly, mm, mm, mm," and then the next person came forward. This musical backing was spontaneous, led by one of the singers I had invited to join us from the African American gospel community. I learned a lot from the way he used the music to hold the space and let the spirit move. It was a lesson in the creative power of cross-pollination and diversity, and in what can happen when we cross the lines of tradition and culture.

R e f l e c t i o n s ◉

The ritual has turned from bemoaning the darkness to affirming the light. It remains for each person to personalize it, to make it stand for something particular in his or her own life, and to move forward with it into the world. Some act of commitment strengthens any ritual or worship experience. In keeping with the motif, it seemed appropriate to initiate a sort of altar call, inviting people to make a personal commitment to their god and a way of life.

This ritual candle lighting was distinct from the candle lighting at the winter solstice, which was performed in silence. That was the time of dormancy. Candlemas is the time that tender shoots appear, and need to be gently tended and encouraged to become strong.

If I had it to do over, I would take a bigger risk with this section of the ritual. I would invite people to step forward to make a commitment to face and speak the truth. (Not Truth with a capital "T"; simply a small-"t" truth, speaking honestly and authentically with everyone we encounter.) I have become convinced that transformation only occurs in the light of truth telling. A radical act would be to call people to risk such a stance in the world. ◐◑

Completion and Commission

We had planned to end the piece as we began it, with an improvisation about going out into the world. At the last minute, however, the improv artist told me she thought that would be superfluous. So instead we allowed the group to form into a circle and sway, singing over and over again the refrain from the song. It was a powerful ending. It bonded people, who definitely left in a different state than the one in which they entered. I said a brief benediction, thanking the forces of earth, air, fire, and water, and the spirit of transformation, commissioning people to go forth carrying the light of the service as the light of the sun grew stronger. People sang "Amen" to the same tune, then went into the social hall for a potluck lunch, as was our habit.

✳ FEMINIST ANALYSIS ✳

What is there to say in analyzing this ritual? The first question we must ask is: Was it feminist? This is a troubling question. There is nothing here that is explicitly feminist, in the way in which we will find it in certain other rituals described in this book (chapters 6, 9, and 10, for example). If we look at the principles proposed by Mary Collins for feminist liturgy, what do we find?

Collins identifies five principles "as basic to intentionally feminist liturgy." The first is that "feminist liturgies ritualize relationships that emancipate and empower women."[7] Nothing in the ritual just described explicitly empowers any particular group; its purpose is to strengthen the community's faith in the transformative power of light, truthfulness, and the turning of the wheel. Is this not, however, of prime relevance for women, who have been silenced in our seeing and speaking? Does this message serve to emancipate and empower women, if it emancipates us to see into the dark corners behind the facades of patriarchy and to clean them up?

There is another way in which this service ritualizes a relationship that emancipates and empowers women: the relationship between women and the divine is mediated through female leadership. More than most rituals in this exploration, this one was a mediated liturgical experience. That is, the congregation's relationship to the sacred was not direct so much as mediated, or interpreted, by the worship leader. The significance of having a strong woman in the role of charismatic preacher should not be overlooked. While we do not, in this service, name that which we address in prayer as either female or male, there is an implicit message in having a woman in the role of intercessor with the divine. Like it or not, the leader carries the image of the holy power. Seeing women, powerful, dynamic, authoritative women, as holy, is emancipating and empowering in the extreme. There is a way in which having a female worship leader is automatically emancipating and empowering to women, unless that leadership is contradicted by the use of male exclusive language for God.

Collins's second principle is that feminist liturgy is the production of the community of worshipers. In this case, while I developed the design with the group of artists hosting the event, I made it a point to have the content emerge from the community as a whole. I sought the resonance between the community and the events occurring in nature which could illuminate our common experience. Much of the content was generated during the ritual directly by the community of worshipers. The design created a form and structure for facilitating, interpreting, and moving the community's content forward. This apparently worked, because people did share group prayers and light candles. It is also noteworthy that there was room for a change in plans when the original design no longer seemed appropriate, and for spontaneous singing as people lit their candles.[8]

Does this ritual critique patriarchal liturgies, as Collins asserts feminist ritual must do? There is certainly nothing overtly critical of traditional male liturgical style in this service; one could even argue that the service is imitative of it. Yet if we look more deeply, we see alterations in form inside the conventional form that imply the kind of criticism Ronald Grimes refers to when he states that all ritual implies criticism of previous rituals.[9]

The room is set in a modified circle, a departure from the traditional church setup, in which preacher and congregation face one another. While we are not in a full circle, which would imply completely shared leadership, there is a "with-ness" to our form that allows for both leadership and fluidity between leader and congregation. The lines are not firmly drawn. There is movement in the shared, central "playing area." The form invites active participation.

Another departure from tradition in this ritual is the use of the body in prayer, implying a radical critique of the patriarchal separation of body and spirit.[10] The opening improvisation, which quite startlingly presents the ordinary and contradictory in the context of the sacred, comes out of a feminist critique of any liturgy in which no room is made for life's ambiguities. Finally, the very theological content of the service and the sermon are a challenge to the image of God as transcendent and unchanging, which historically has gone hand in hand with a patriarchal worldview. So while there was no overt intent to critique patriarchal liturgy, the mere existence of such an experimental worship event implies some need that is not being met in conventional Sunday-morning services, at least for this small community.

In her final point, Collins notes the absence of text in feminist ritual, observing that such ritualizing is generated at the level of practice. But, she notes, this may be a strategy rather than a principle, and might change as the production of feminist ritual and liturgy becomes less of a novelty.[11] I would argue that texts are gradually being written as feminists ritualists grow into the seriousness of our project. Indeed this is one of them. These texts are intended as critical examinations of a new form, or guides, at most. They are not, I hope, intended as scripts to be followed by rote but as ideas to be explored, or perhaps processes to be adapted for other uses. If it is to be effective, ritual action is always particular to the group and setting. While the above ritual actions and content could be used as a pattern for another liturgist or group, the fabric of the ritual would need to be theirs in order to fit the particulars of their setting.

While some feminists doing ritual may be operating exclusively inside feminist, womanist, and mujerista communities, most of us are not. For a variety of reasons, many feminists leading ritual and worship are operating inside mixed groups, at least part of the time. It is neither possible nor desirable to only address the explicit needs only of women cum women. Nor can feminist worship leaders always be seen as grinding some feminist axe, preaching week after week on the feminist soapbox. There are other issues that arise from the community, as well as from the seasonal calendar. It is worth grappling with the question of how it is possible to operate inside the commitments of feminism while producing liturgies that serve the entire community.

It does not serve the cause of women to leave our feminism at the door of mixed worship, applying feminist principles only to Woman Church events or the event of a special women's service. If women continue to do so, feminist ritual will never move beyond the separatist women's ghetto. It is high time to move feminist ritual and liturgy away from the liturgical margins and into the mainstream. While there is value in women-only groups for support, visioning, and healing, the need for feminist proactivity remains when men enter the group or when the subject matter is not focused on gender-specific concerns. Feminism is a way of seeing the world that informs our every thought process and action. If feminist principles are to take on a transformative function rather than a merely critical one, they must inform all ritual and liturgical events.

Perhaps it is time to broaden the definition of feminist ritual. If one were to include in the definition all ritual that reflects a female/process notion of the sacred, all ritual that models powerful female leadership, includes shared leadership and participation, and expands the definition of the sacred to include women's experience of the everyday and of their bodies, one would have a feminist model for all seasons. This model, informed and shaped by feminism's values and critique, could engage all areas of common ritual life. I would assert that this is the next phase of what is needed ritually to empower and emancipate women.

Did this ritual accomplish its stated purpose? Did people leave with renewed faith in the light's power to transform life? As no follow-up was done, I can speak with certainty only for myself. This ritual was a personal turning point in my life. I performed this ritual at a time when my life, like February, was bare and bleak. I was dealing with health concerns, my professional life was at a standstill, and my marriage was in trouble.

As a result of grappling with the subject matter of denial and truth telling, addressing the many excuses for lying, I noticed that I had the same reasons as the tobacco companies or Dow Corning for deceiving others: they can't take the truth; I can't take the consequences. I decided that in the long run, denial and deception do not serve my values. I decided as a result of preaching the above homily to thereafter tell the truth and deal with the consequences in all instances. I made a public vow, joined by three others, before all spirits assembled there, that I would no longer make up excuses or use justifications for lying to anyone for any reason ever again.

It was a frightening thing to do, and it required great faith. It has forced me to clean up all sorts of messes in my life, even old student loans and parking tickets. It has simplified and generally improved my personal and professional relationships. So at least for me, that little bit of light shone down past all my fears. As I looked into the dark corners of my life, owned up to them, and swept them away, one by one, my life was transformed from the Beast into Beauty.

CAKES FOR THE QUEEN OF HEAVEN

✳

The Spring Equinox

Writing this as I am, three weeks before the longest night of the year, I cannot help but wonder, was it ever spring? Will it ever be so again? A vague memory lingers, made of clichès. Are there really fragrant flowers? Do purple lupine really line the mountains in the California desert? Do the hillsides actually turn that radiant green that only lasts for a moment before turning to straw in the summer sun?

From winter we could not imagine it if we had not seen it. Spring's beauty is as surprising, as innocent and ephemeral as a young maiden awakening. Soon she will blossom, we can see, but for the moment she is shy and full of promise, the bud on the branch whose color and fullness we may only guess at and not yet know. Yet she is so bold! Spring behaves as though she were invincible, such is the recklessness of innocence, broadcasting seductive fragrances with abandon! She holds within her the promise of warmth and summer, of arms full of fruit and riotously colored summer vegetables. But it is only the promise, not the fulfillment. Would she be so brazen if she knew what lay ahead?

Herein lies the mystery of maids and vegetation: in the flowering seed sleeps the knowledge and the promise of maturity. If someone were to tell us, as we gazed upon an apple blossom in April, that the flower will make way for fruit, which will fall by the tree, to be consumed by an animal who will take the seed into its bowels, transporting it miles away to lie fertilized on another ground, where it will grow into yet another flowering, fruiting tree, how would we believe them? This is the mystery of springtime. In every flower returning from the land of the dead lies this promise.

This was the promise that pilgrims celebrated in the city of Eleusis for two thousand unbroken years, the mystery of mother grain and daughter seed, known as Demeter and Persephone. These well-known rites marked the turning from summer to autumn (the autumnal equinox), and from winter to spring (the vernal equinox). The Eleusinian mysteries will probably always remain shrouded in the secrecy that was maintained for as long as they were performed, but we do know they told the story of Persephone's abduction to the underworld in the fall, and her return to her mother in the spring.

Myths are multilayered in their meanings. It is likely that this allegory of the natural mystery of life's awakening, ripening, death, and rebirth also had layers of significance alluding to the political machinations of the Greek pantheon, where the new, patriarchal gods led by Zeus had to fight it out with the old, indigenous goddess Demeter. In the classic version of the story, as it has come down to us in the Homeric Hymn, Demeter and her beloved daughter must eventually accept Persephone's forced marriage and her annual sojourn in the underworld, just as life must accept death in order for rebirth to occur. While explaining nature's death and rebirth cycles, the myth served also to justify the patriarchal rise to power and Demeter's uneasy compromise with it.[1]

The Greek myths are interesting to us not just because they hold some essential truths about nature, but because our culture is the descendant of patriarchal Greek culture. Its stories and values live in our social arrangements, our institutions, our religious symbols, and our own psyches, shaped as they are by patriarchal acculturation patterns.[2] The story of the young goddess helplessly abducted from her mother and taken far away to live in her husband's world is not a pretty or an easy story for feminists. It does not empower women; it does, however, reflect many centuries of women's experience. Our purpose in reviving it for a feminist celebration was neither to sanitize the story nor to dwell in it, but to reclaim and redeem it.

We chose this myth, then, for two reasons: (1) because the date of the public celebration had been set to coincide with the vernal equinox, when Persephone's return had traditionally been celebrated, and (2) it was a useful mythic template for our theme of return to the Mother, meaning return to a female image of divine authority. In using a story that has been enacted many times but having feminists redeem it, we were deliberately stepping inside an existing resonance pattern and altering its mythic future.

In redeeming such a deeply archetypal story, we aimed to redeem our experience as women, for all women are Persephone. We have all been locked in patriarchy's hell, exiled from our Mother, for the past five thousand years. Where we do not reclaim and transform our mythic background and our painful past, we continue to live out of it. When we ignore it, it continues to inform the background of our every action and thought. In the ritual that follows, a myth that was probably originally redacted to justify and mirror the increasing rule of the fathers and the diminished role of the Grain Mother[3] is reversed, turned on its head. Women reclaim it for their own purposes, enter it, and alter its future. In bringing it into the present, women can appropriate a myth without attempting to change its past, instead making its symbols their own to serve the cause of their own liberation.

We present our myth as a story that is happening now, in which the participants have a role to play. The tale of Persephone and Demeter is not just an archaic tale told of some ancient time and place. The saga of the archetypal mother and daughter torn from one another continues today. At last women are reclaiming our source of life and power. What better day to do it than the day of Persephone's traditional return, the spring equinox? In claiming the female face of the divine, we are all returning to our Mother and to ourselves. In the story of Persephone's return, we find a symbol for our own return to our estranged Mother. The communion of the ancient cakes, described in chapter 1, would seal our troth.

✳ THE RITUAL ✳

This ritual, then, is a model of feminist appropriation, transformation, and/or redemption of three central symbols used to religiously empower women from mixed traditions in a feminist ritual for the spring equinox. The three symbols are:

1. Cakes for the Queen of Heaven, from the passage in Jeremiah, commonly a symbol of women's betrayal of the Hebrew god, described at length in chapter 1.
2. The rite of communion, usually associated with the Christian faith, which we reclaimed.
3. The mother/daughter archetype as exemplified in the "lesser" mysteries of Demeter and Persephone, which we used to redeem and restore our relationship to the divine female and our own female genealogy.

This ritual was designed to also serve as a teaching tool for my class in feminist ritual and liturgy, which would follow the public presentation. Therefore I paid special attention to demonstrating certain key elements of ritual in its construction: juxtaposition of familiarity and surprise, the use of rhythm, color, and movement, the use of different learning styles through engaging all the senses, and theatrically effective ritual production and performance, as we shall see. I also carefully followed the traditional order, or liturgy, making sure that all the steps and pieces were both present and discernible.

The task before us was to craft an experience for women of different backgrounds and faith traditions by which they would arrive at a pivotal moment, ready to claim their power and heritage as women by reclaiming the ancient symbol of the mother goddess. The story of Persephone's return to her mother was the story line and mythic framework. The cakes were the central symbol, marking the affirmation of our own female legacy and tradition. How would we move a group of a hundred (mostly) women from here to there? We would have to pass through some stages to arrive at such a momentous turning. I have included the entire "script" for this ritual, as it was written and performed by Diane Darling and me, because it so clearly demonstrates certain liturgical principles and procedures. The opening section follows.

Gathering and Creating Sacred Space

Setting: Room is set with chairs in circle (three concentric circles in spiral), outlined in barley (the grain said to be sacred to the mother goddess, Demeter) and flowers (symbol of the maiden goddess, Persephone). Low coffee table covered with spring green cloth becomes an altar in center of circle. Natural, nontoxic incense and a white candle are burning on the east altar, as people are ushered clockwise through east gate (east is the symbol of new beginnings and spring, for it is where the sun rises).

Greeting: Guests greeted and led to seats, inner circle first, by official greeters.

Gathering: Clapping and singing. "She's Been Waiting" led by Wendy. Diane walks outside perimeter of outer circle drumming downbeat.

Part One

Canto: She's been waiting, waiting
Response: She's been waiting, waiting

Canto: She's been waiting so long
Response: She's been waiting so long

Canto: She's been waiting for Her children
Response: She's been waiting for Her children
Canto: to remember
Response: to remember
(Repeat entire verse before moving to Part Two)

Part Two

Canto: Blessed be and blessed are the lovers of the Lady
Response: Blessed be and blessed are the lovers of the Lady
Canto: Blessed be and blessed are Maiden, Mother, Crone
Response: Blessed be and blessed are Maiden, Mother, Crone
Canto: Blessed be and blessed are the ones who sing together
Response: Blessed be and blessed are the ones who sing together
Canto: Blessed be and blessed are the ones who sing alone.
Response: Blessed be and blessed are the ones who sing alone.[4]
(Repeat Parts One and Two to end, 10–15 minutes, as people are getting seated. End with "She's been waiting for Her children to remember . . . to return." At end strike Tibetan bowl.)

Cast Circle: (Wendy passes bell bowl to preappointed person at east altar, and walks inner circle clockwise, as congregants rise and hold hands. Diane walks outer perimeter with wand, echoing key phrases.)

1. We are here today in the circle of community, where we are together as equals, safe and respected. The circle is cast once. *(Gong)*
2. We are held in the circle of the life cycle, the circle of the arms of the Great Mother, who embraces us with her abundance. The circle is cast twice. *(Throw barley around circle. Gong)*
3. As long as we are on this earth, we are within the sacred circle of her womb, the womb that gives us life and then takes us back when we are finished with this life. The circle is cast thrice. *(Strew flower petals around from basket. Gong)*

Song (all sing): "A circle is cast again and again and again, and a . . ."[5] *(Repeat in round until an auditory circle fills the room containing everyone in it.)*

Reflections

We began as usual, by casting a circle. But there was the gathering, even before that. The way we gather for a sacred ceremony sets a tone. I wanted the participants to feel comfortable and engaged from the very beginning. Knowing that many of our attendees would be women who attend church regularly, I thought it important to bridge the worship styles. I have always regarded the custom of having ushers escort worshipers to their seats a gracious one. Why not have officials of the institution, known and respected by their community, greet people and escort them into the circle of chairs. By that means we accomplished three things: (1) making the guests feel welcome and served, (2) connecting our unfamiliar actions with customs and people who were known and familiar, and (3) making sure that people walked around instead of through the circle, thereby creating the form and distributing themselves around it.

I wanted people to be aware immediately that they were in a participatory ritual, not a spectator sport. What better way than to get them singing? I have found that in many African American churches singing begins as much as half an hour before the formal service. This brings people bodily into a common celebration. It also allays anxiety by giving guests something to do while waiting for latecomers. Finally, it raises the energy, or, in show business talk, "warms up" the crowd. I chose a simple song with a heavy downbeat, one that I could line out in the tradition of the old spiritual so that everyone could simply follow line by line to participate.[6] I clapped, and made eye contact with all the guests, encouraging them to clap and sing along. Diane beat it out on the drum, repeating the same verses over and over until everyone knew them and was singing gustily. Where there had been a collection of individuals, a worshiping community began to form.

Once everyone was seated, it was time to enclose the group in a sacred space, typically a circle. A circle is egalitarian; everyone can see one another, and important actions can take place inside a contained space. Ritual must have boundaries to be safe and powerful. These may be defined in a number of different ways, so long as they resonate in the archetypes accessible to the worshiping body.

Because of the size of the crowd, we made three concentric circles in what was really more of a spiraling egg shape, defined by one border of flowers for Persephone and another of barley for Demeter.

The reader will observe that the circle was cast in all four learning styles:

Visually, as described above with flowers and barley
Kinesthetically, by holding hands
Auditorily, with the sound of the Tibetan bowl being hit and allowed to reverberate, and with the singing of a round
Verbally/cognitively, with the words used above

Every ritual action should resonate on as many levels as possible to have real experiential impact. Finally, we all held hands and sang our declaration (auditory, verbal, and kinesthetic) that indeed a circle was cast which connected our ritual actions to the ritual actions of all who went before us, strengthening the resonance further through the singing of a circular song, a round. ❧

Invoking Ourselves into Presence with the Sacred

Call Directions: Each caller steps forward in turn and faces her direction before speaking. Others follow.

East. From the East comes the dawn of new possibilities, the sunrise, and the spring air fragrant with flowers. We call on the spirit of the air to blow away our fears and all ill will from the past, to allow us to breathe free. *(All take deep breath. Priestess fans air with bird wing.)*

South: From the South we call on the warmth of the sun growing stronger daily to strengthen us as women. Let our power and fire grow and shine alongside it, illuminating and enlivening us. *(Priestess lights candle at center altar.)*

West: From the West comes the wild indomitable ocean, mother of all life on earth, and the cool, refreshing waters of the running stream. Be with us today as the wild tempestuous mother, and as the daughter who always runs to meet her. *(Priestess turns rain stick [a Mesoamerican instrument that makes the sound of rain falling].)*

North: Solid as a rock you lie beneath us. Without you, we are not. Come to us from the North, flesh and bones of our Mother Earth, with your enduring strength. Be with us. Ground our being in your fertile transformations. *(All stomp feet on ground.)*

Reflections

It is customary in many traditions, from Native American to South American to Old European to Chinese, to call on the fundamental elements of life to be part of sacred ceremony. It is not abstract, unmoving spirit that holds the sacred, but the basic elements of life in the physical universe, earth, air, fire, and water or, in the Chinese system, wood, metal, fire, air, and water. I use the four elements of the old European (and Native American) models because I believe them to be more familiar and accessible to the Western mind. They are a way of calling in a diversity of qualities (embodied in the elements) to inform the rite and to honor the sacred in the physical world. This is also the beginning of calling the participants into deeper presence by inviting them to breathe (see East invocation) and feel the ground (North invocation.) Having participants present in their bodies is a key, I believe, to people's experiencing any potentially powerful experience. Please note, as in casting the circle, the use of the kinesthetic approach, in the stomping and breathing, the visual in the lighting of the candle, and the auditory in the use of the rain stick, as well as the verbal approach of the spoken word. The allusions are also congruent with the season of spring, which we are celebrating here.

It can take time to encourage inexperienced people to call an element in a manner that embodies it, but it is worth it. Not only does it give more people a role in the ritual, so that it becomes the product of the worshiping body; it lends the power of diverse voices to the common project.[7] It should be pointed out, however, that the calls must be powerful, genuine, and loud enough to hear. The purpose of invoking is to bring out particular elemental energies and qualities, to bring congregants to a heightened awareness of the sacred, and to raise up particular elements appropriate to the rite and its purposes. It is for this reason that all the invocations in this ritual relate to power and freedom for women, embodied in the mother/daughter relationship, which is central to the theme.

Exposition: Why We Are Here

PRIESTESS: Please be seated and welcome. Welcome to our circle. Welcome to our celebration of spring and our long-awaited return to our Mother. Perhaps you know that a long time ago all people honored the Divine Mother. They called her by many names—Asherah, AnaHita, Spider Woman, Teteo Innan, Demeter, and other names we do not remember and probably could not pronounce. Throughout the world and for many thousands of years, people believed they were *born* into this life from the sacred body of the Divine Mother. Imagine. Imagine believing you were conceived, not in sin separate from God, but in the womb of God, the Mother of all life. That would mean that your body is sacred, too.

Then, over a period of thousands of years, the fathers took over. The sons became arrogant. The Goddess was forced to go into exile. Women were burned at the stake or stoned for even mentioning her name. And still she has been faithfully waiting.

She's been waiting so long for her children to remember. She's been waiting so long for her daughters. She's been waiting for centuries, millennia! She's been waiting while the Father has been raging in his pride and false independence, his so-called freedom from her demands, conquering her body again and again, all the while pretending he does not need it, taking her children, and claiming that he alone could make life!

For so long we have been Motherless children! We almost forgot the Beloved One who gave us our birth, the One at whose body we nurse still. Almost . . .

Yet in this first moment of spring, we are remembering again. Gathered together on the knife's edge that cuts between dark and light, we see new life budding and rising from her body. We have the power to remember. We can awaken as though from a long sleep. We can shake the cobwebs of patriarchy from our heads. And like Persephone emerging from Hades, we can return.

We are here today to honor and return to the Mother.

(Song: "Return Again" to sing Persephone in.)

Return again, return again, return to the land of your [birth]. *(Repeat)*

Return to what you are, return to who you are, return to where you are born and born again.

Return again, return, return to the land of your [birth].[8]

Reflections

Once people are gathered in a group they want to have some idea of what is going to happen. This is especially important with groups unfamiliar with this style of worship and who may have some concern as to whether their standards and values will be respected. It is the job of the leader or priestess to put their fears to rest by her powerful, respectful presence and words, without going into a lengthy explanation or apologia. The language of story, in myth and metaphor, serves best to include participants and to evoke in them a powerful relationship with the ritual events.

The ritual purpose, or at least its overt, conscious purpose, needs to be stated simply and clearly (e.g., "We are here to honor and return to the Mother"), so that everyone present is in alignment with it. This should be spoken in language consistent with the ritual event or story, as demonstrated below. Well-wrought symbols rooted in nature and in the body speak for themselves, and do not need explanation!

In the section above we set a context of the history of women's religious symbols, asking each woman to imagine personally how seeing the female as divine would alter her view of the world and herself. We speak in broad poetic sweeps of the historical, religious movements that removed the Goddess from our consciousness, telling the story with images to which all women can relate. We speak of our loneliness; all women can feel the plight of motherless children. We continue throughout this section to refer to the motif set by the opening song, of her waiting for us to remember. Then we present the special opportunity that today is, the reason we have gathered them here. This sets the scene for Persephone to speak for us all. ◎⌒

Investment: Engaging the Congregation

PERSEPHONE *(entering circle from the East):*
Six lifetimes ago I was my Mother's Daughter,
A free Earth Goddess roaming free fields.
Rape subdued me, starvation broke me.
I lost the fruits of the Earth for six blood-sweet seeds . . .[9]
PRIESTESS: But surely you all know the story.
PERSEPHONE: *My* story.
PRIESTESS: *Our* story. For we are all Persephone. We have all been torn from our Mother. We have all been raped and broken. You remember.
PERSEPHONE: Oh yes. You remember, don't you? *(Goes out to women in circle, as if reminding them of a shared experience.)* We were young and very full of ourselves. The whole world bloomed under our eyes. Perhaps we thought we didn't need our Mother. We thought nothing could harm us. We were invincible.
We wandered away. Then he arrived with his narcissus flowers, his fast chariot, his warrior gods, his promises and his threats. We tried to get away. Or we were too frightened to say no. Or maybe we thought we'd show her. Or that we could change him.
He had made a deal with our father, in the back room, of course, for the use of our bodies and the power of our minds, in exchange for . . . what? Money? Power? Survival? We were never told. He took us far away from our Mother, our sisters, our community.
PRIESTESS *(addressing congregants):* You remember. What was YOUR story? How did patriarchy happen to you? Bind your thread to Persephone. When was the moment? What happened?

(A few women share extemporaneously. For example:"Two men came in through the bedroom window, I thought it was the cats making such a clatter. They took me against my will. No one believed me." "I was told I could not be a priest when I grew up." "I was told it was a sin to love another woman," etc.)

Reflections

It is at this point that the ritual becomes explicitly feminist. It names patriarchy, but does not leave it in the abstract. It asks: How did this happen to Persephone? Then it goes further by asking each woman to reflect on her own particular experience of it, her own loss of innocence: How did it happen to you? Persephone includes all women's experience inside her own archetypal experience. The purpose here was to elicit women's outrage, to turn up the volume on the intensity of the experience, and to personalize it. What occurred was powerful. Woman stood up and shared. Some shared things they had never before spoken aloud. Others shared things they had spoken before, but had never understood as more than personal, sanctified in the context of sacred story. We were all goddesses and sisters, recalling our defilement at the hands of strangers and lovers, institutions and authority figures.

Purgation

PRIESTESS: When our Mother found out, she was inconsolable. She roamed the earth searching for someone who could tell her where her beloved daughter had gone. She had counted on us for so many things, and she had such dreams for us! But everyone was afraid to tell her. Everyone was afraid to speak. He had such power! When one who had seen finally spoke, it was to tell her that the one who had stolen us was a fitting husband! Imagine!

So the Mother of All Life disguised herself (remember?) as an ugly old woman. Perhaps some thought her to be a witch. And she waited in her temple, refusing to rejoin the other gods without her daughter, refusing to allow anything to grow until her daughter was returned to her.

PERSEPHONE: We were locked away in hell for a long time. A season? A year? Five thousand years? It was so long that sometimes we forgot that we had ever been free. We began to think our life there was all there was. We became resigned. We ate the food that was available to us—pomegranate seeds kept us alive, even while condemning us to be bound by the fruits of hell.

When we eat the fruits of oppression, we become bound by it. We begin to think we need it, like thinking we deserve to be abused, or thinking we need the goods that are produced in misery, or the ones that destroy our Mother Earth. We need our abusive spouse, our Styrofoam cups, our redwood decks, our Nikes produced by the sweat of Asian women, and our children's toys produced by the sweatshop labor of other children. It was the same long ago when we turned our heads as our African sisters became enslaved. We ate the fruits of their hell. Such is the nature of oppression. We become party to it.

PRIESTESS *(to congregants):* Bind your thread to Persephone. How have you become party to oppression? *(A few women share extemporaneously. For example: "I stayed for a long time after he beat me because I was afraid to go out on my own." "I hit my children." "I wear clothes made by women in sweatshops," etc.)*

Reflections

The first speech in the above section addresses people's fear of speaking out in the face of powerful authority, how we rationalize rather than confront its abuses. The narrative goes on to tell of silence, isolation, hiding, disguising one's power and beauty in resistance, refusing to serve injustice. This was the story of the Mother. It is often the story of the witch, the wise woman, the lesbian, the spinster, the madwoman. The daughter's story is more complex.

She describes the normalization of oppression, the resignation that gives birth to collusion and even collaboration. Women are not outside the system that suppresses us. We consume its goods, eat its fruit, all the while being poisoned by it. Until we, yes, confess our complicity with patriarchy, we shall never break its bonds, and we will find ourselves ensnared in denial and addiction to its fruits.

It was risky to ask women to share so revealingly in a group of relative strangers. This was far riskier than the sharing of our very personal pain and outrage. It required revealing to one another and to ourselves a shameful moment of selling out. I was not at all sure that anyone would speak. But I hoped the bond we had formed in the earlier sharing would be strong and flexible enough to allow some women to come forward. They did, with powerful confessions of covering up for battering spouses, remaining in abusive relationships and jobs, due to fear. They spoke of betraying mothers and daughters, as well as themselves. A man present also shared. They shared their cowardice, and by so doing, created an opening for courage.

This piece of the liturgy is troublesome for many feminists and Neopagans. We have been so beaten down with guilt and shame that we would rather turn away altogether from anything that smacks of confession, any implication of complicity, for fear of being crushed in the rush to blame the victim (as occurred in much of the literature on co-dependence, in which women, as co-addicts, were being blamed for addiction, or victims of battering were faulted, in a twisted misuse of Jungian analysis, for causing their partners' abuse). While we do not wish to be a party to this practice, we do wish to empower women. Seeing ourselves entirely as victims does not serve us. We must acknowledge not cause, but cooperation, with our subordinators. In acknowledging and owning our complicity, we empower ourselves to eschew such complicity and reclaim power in our lives, despite what we fear may be the consequences.

There is a ritual reason, as well, that I include a purgation, or confessional piece, in most rituals. Just as clearing away the rocks from the soil is a necessary step to make room for the planting of new seeds in the spring, purgation creates a clearing for the planting of a new possibility or commitment. ❧

The Turning: Claiming and Empowering a Central Symbol

PERSEPHONE: But even when I thought I forgot, there was something calling to me from the far reaches of memory: I missed my mother. Now the day is waxing longer, and in the sky tonight the old moon is waxing new. And today, the first day of spring, we have the opportunity to return to life. Persephone emerges from her shadowed realm, and into the sunlight of Demeter's joy.

PRIESTESS *(to congregants):* Every year your mother waits.

PERSEPHONE: Of course, Hades hopes we will forget. In fact, he counts on it. He tries to slip us fresh pomegranate seeds every year, so that we will stay. Sometimes we do. But I miss my mother.

PRIESTESS: That is why we are here together on this day. In the circle of community. To remember to return. We are all together on this day of Persephone's return. At last we have the courage to set a different pattern for all women in all seasons. We can restore our beloved Mother to her place of honor among us.

PERSEPHONE *(to congregants):* Are we willing to return to our Mother in this season of our lives? *(Group whispers yes)* Are we willing to open our hearts to her and smile Persephone's smile in her embrace? *(Group again whispers yes).* And will we look for her in every woman, searching every face for her divine light, however dim or veiled? Can we really do that? Is it time? Are you willing?

ALL *(Whispers rising to crescendo):* Yes!

PRIESTESS: There is an ancient way that women used to honor the Mother. They baked cakes. Sometimes and in some places they called them cakes to the Queen of Heaven, and they would make offerings of them to the Goddess. *(Persephone gets cakes from central altar, holds tray for all to see.)*

This is the recipe they used *(takes appropriate bowls from altar)*: Barley which was sacred to Asherah, the Hebrew Goddess, and to Demeter, Persephone's mother, honey for sweetness, fragrant coriander seeds, precious raisins and figs, mixed with milk and curds of goats, then set to rise with a wild strain of yeast begun in Egypt six thousand years ago, and baked slowly with safflower oil. They ate them

under the new moon, and so they made them in that shape. Into themselves they took grain and sun, heaven and earth, made one with their own life-giving flesh, as we do tonight. I made them for us. See? This is a very special moment. It may be the first time these cakes have been eaten and offered in thousands of years. As we eat them, we connect with the ancient matriarchs and priestesses.
Let us bless the cakes.
Blessing Song *(All sing while two volunteers take cakes around circle for all to bless)*
We all come from the Goddess, and to her we shall return,
Like a drop of rain, flowing to the ocean. [10]

Reflections

Every ritual of transformation has a turning point, where the direction of the ritual turns from the sin or sorrow of the past to the opportunity in the present to stand for a new future. This ritual turns not on the central archetypal figures, but on the participants themselves, who are offered the power to reclaim for themselves and for all women what was lost long ago and by each subsequent generation. They are called on to recognize the Goddess "in every woman, searching every face for her divine light, however dim or veiled." In a rising crescendo of affirmations they agree. They have the power. They bless the cakes with a chant that says yes, indeed we are her children, born of her to return to her.

Empowering Our Magic

PERSEPHONE: I lost the fruits of the Earth for six blood-sweet seeds.
But now I am rising from darkness and despair.
Like the phoenix from flame, like Aphrodite from foam
I am rising from the earth green as the spring, and singing.

I have dwelt in the land of the dead, yet still I live.
I have ruled in hell, yet still I am divine.
I was locked in the underworld of mad civilizations.
I am overcoming it.
I am bursting the twigs,
swelling the buds,
unraveling the petals.
I am again my mother's daughter
A free earth goddess, roaming free fields. [11]

(Priestess offers cake to Persephone.)

PERSEPHONE *(taking cake)*:

I, Persephone, daughter of Demeter, daughter of Rhea, daughter of Gaia, do honor the Mother.

(Persephone takes cake, lights cauldron, and drops in a cake. All stand. Begin drum and rattle. Priestess begins toning on "MA," increasing in power and volume until room is vibrating with a unity and intensity of intention.)

R e f l e c t i o n s

Ideally there should be a transformational climax in every ritual. Everything preceding it leads up to it, and everything following it derives from it. The climactic moment of this rite of reunion and dedication is the moment in which we, as a group, join the women of Jeremiah in their defiant act of commitment to the Goddess of their ancestors.

Combining two traditions, with Persephone speaking for all of us as her daughter, we make a burnt offering to the Queen of Heaven. We take the first cake from the basket and place it into the fire, while raising power on the sound of "MA," the primal syllable meaning mother in virtually every language. It is a terrifying moment. Will lightning strike us for honoring the female divine in this ancient manner?

Why do this? Why choose this symbolic action as opposed to some other, less charged one? First, because of its drama. One must not neglect the theatrical work of liturgy. Drama is essential if ritual is to work transformationally on the participants. Without drama, ritual actions serve merely as signs of nice ideas, as is frequently the case in commonly occurring ritual acts.[12] It is for this reason that primal ritual often includes a shocking act, breaking some taboo or revealing some surprise at its climax. It is by this act and the drama surrounding it (note the drum and rattle that accent the act of offering) that we wake up the brain through a powerful emotional response so that we deeply assimilate the symbol and the shift it implies.[13]

A second reason for this act is the resonance it holds. Each time we repeat a ritual act that has been done before, we are connecting ourselves and our actions to those who have gone before us. This is why it is preferable to reclaim and appropriate existing symbols instead of making them up from whole cloth. Sometimes, it is true, we must invent from nothing, but better to stand on the shoulders of our forebears when we do so.

There is yet another reason for the action we take. It lies in the realm of magic. We are actually making an offering to the force beyond our comprehension that we call the Goddess, the Mother, the Life Force, the Queen of Heaven. We do not pretend to understand this act, or how, why, or even if it "works."

There is an impulse to honor, to worship, to offer the first and the best of what we have to that Source of All, however we name it, through sacrifice. It is an impulse older than any single tradition, and is found in all of them. In this symbolic act, we recognize our dependence on the force that is greater, and pay it homage. We step beyond our separate egos and rededicate ourselves to the greater whole. ❧

Communion and Dedication: Committing Ourselves

(Persephone offers basket to Priestess.)
PERSEPHONE: Who would like to declare herself in honoring the Mother in ourselves and our ancestors, as far back as we can remember? Please come forward. Take a cake and speak your name followed by the name of your mother, then her mother, and so on.
PRIESTESS *(steps forward and takes cake from Persephone)*: I, Wendy, daughter of Jane, daughter of Evelyn, daughter of Bettie, daughter of Jane, do honor the Mother.
(Other women come forward as in an altar call. They are lined up at the microphone, where the priestess dispenses the cakes one at a time to every woman who wishes to partake. It is riveting as each woman walks forward and claims her heritage, speaking the names of her mothers and her children. PERSEPHONE drums quietly, to hold the energy, until every woman who wishes to has had the opportunity to eat and speak. Finally DIANE takes a cake, and this time eats it, proclaiming her own biological lineage, removing the persona of Persephone.)
PRIESTESS *(prayer)*: Mother, you need wait no longer. We are here. We have remembered to return. We eat of your sacred body, we drink from your sacred well. We shall never again forget you. We proclaim ourselves daughters of the Great Mother.

Song:　Listen listen listen to my heart's song
　　　　Listen listen listen to my heart's song
　　　　We will always be with you, we will always remember,
　　　　We will always be with you, we will always remember. *(Repeat)*[14]

As the final song mirrors and responds to the request and longing of the first song, we assert that her children have indeed remembered, and shall always remember.

Reflections

Communion is a powerful act of affirming connection because it is an act of embodying, assimilating a symbol bodily. These moon-shaped cakes are the symbol of our union with the Mother. We could easily say, "This is my body which is given for you," and literally have it be true. No need for doctrines of transubstantiation: the grain goddess is the grain and the earth from which it grows. The Mother gives of her own body to all her children.

There are those who would say that this is an insensitive appropriation of Christian communion. I would argue that communion is as old as bread, and that the sacred baking and eating of it ceremonially goes back to the early grain-producing cultures, where the first loaf was always offered to the reigning deity. By eating of the cakes, we seal the pact: participants are connecting with their female ancestors, spiritual and biological, and affirming the Divine Mother within all of us. ◉◢

Completion and Commission: Take Down and Send Forth

PRIESTESS: We have done our work. On this first day of spring, when the moon and sun are waxing and the comet passes on its twenty-thousand-year journey through our sky, we have tipped the balance in a different direction. Now it is time to take the power we have raised into the world, reborn with the spring. Don't be too surprised if you find yourself feeling stronger or more loved. Don't be surprised if in the months to come you see women's power growing all around you. We go forth with the blessings of the Mother, for she is always in us and all around us.

PERSEPHONE *(takes down elements from center, turning to appropriate direction, then moves to outer circle, walks counterclockwise, opposite Priestess)*

PRIESTESS: As the womb opens to release us to the Mother's embrace, the circle is open once. *(Gong)*

As her embrace opens to release us into loving community, the circle is open twice. *(Gong)*

As our community opens to release us to share what we have learned with the larger world, the circle is open thrice. *(Gong)*

Still we rest in the web of her weaving, the circle from which we cannot fall, the great embrace of space, and thus we say: "The circle is open but unbroken. Merry meet and merry part and merry meet again."[15] *(Final gong)*

R e f l e c t i o n s ✿

This final section was constructed to be a bookend to the opening section. It is the epilogue, the denouement of the ritual work that we have done. We complete it and send forth our energy into the world. This is critical if our work is not to be a mere feel-good experience for the people present. We declare that we have tipped the balance in a different direction from a five-thousand-year trend. Our assertions have the power of our collective word and will. We further assert that what has happened here will send ripples into the world in the coming months; such is the nature of magic. Then we open the circle, using the same images in reverse that we used in the beginning, creating a symmetry of expanding circles from womb to arms, to community and world, making sure the congregation realizes that our magic does not stop here, but goes forth with them into the larger world of their influence.

❋ FEMINIST ANALYSIS ❋

After thousands of years of forgetting, we have remembered to return. In the critical moment we miraculously snatched Persephone from the hands of her abductor and restored the mother/daughter bond. We defied the fathers' orders and ate of the sacred cakes. JHWH and Hades were seen walking off together in angry disbelief, no doubt to commiserate over a beer. Score one for feminism. The daughter is free, and the mother is no longer bereft. But neither is Persephone the same maiden as she was before it all happened, as her mother no doubt found out. She can no more return to her former innocence than the apple blossom can, after it has been picked. She was plucked from her home and taken far away, and she is now Hades' queen, as well as her mother's daughter.

None of us can be the same as we were before our abduction to hell. Too much has happened. We have been ravaged, broken, and raped. We cannot go back in time or myth to undo the damage. But even Demeter cannot remain in bitter mourning forever, and it is time for mother and daughter to reemerge together in victory. While we cannot undo the injuries of the past, we can redeem them. And redeem them we do, by bringing them into the present, claiming them as our own, releasing our shame, and writing a new ending to an old story. In the moment when the sun crossed the equator to grow stronger in our hemisphere, briefly balancing the day and the night, women reclaimed their ancient heritage and wholeness, their union with the Mother.

This is the all-important covenant we seal with our communion: the return of the daughter to the mother. Why does this matter? How does it give women access to our power?

While we are not all mothers, we are all daughters of mothers. The Mother is the first symbol and the first power we encounter in our preverbal lives. She is the great All That Is, our original Goddess. Good mother or bad mother, her body is still the source of our life; we swim and are nourished in her warm, underground seas of darkness for nine months. She does not occur initially for us as a person, but as an archetype—all-encompassing, all-powerful, the terrifying and multivalent being on whose love and whims we depend for our very survival, she who feeds us at her own breast. She does not become a person for us until much later, if ever. Her acceptance is the first act of grace our young lives know, her rejection is life threatening. Our memory of this act is eternal. It does not go away, no matter how we may turn from it.

Later we flee from this dependency and the dependency that the archetype evokes in us. We pretend that we are free, or opt instead for the more distant relationship with a Father god. But there is a cost. In this act of rejecting the Mother, we reject ourselves, our own dark power and the power of life itself. She is always there, in our deepest cells' memories, waiting for us to remember. The archetype of our earliest body recollections calls to us and points us toward the eternal embodied one. All of us know the Divine Mother. All of us can remember. And remember we do. In spite of all the social influences and patriarchal cultural overlays, she is there beneath them, waiting.[16]

Once again this ritual shows itself to be a project of feminist archaeology, in which we dig through the surface layers of patriarchal myth and our own ancestry to find the Ancient Mother in the cave beneath. In accepting and reclaiming her, we are reclaiming life and our own power, just as Persephone does in her return. We are owning and choosing that from which we cannot escape, can only in our hubris deny: the dark, wild powerful force of birth and death, overwhelming and terrifying, yet comforting and freeing in our surrender to it. We wonder, "Why was I running all these years from her, from my deepest self, the Goddess whose body I mirror?" One profound outcome of this ritual was women's reports of body memories calling back a connection they had long forgotten, and honoring and rejoicing in it.

FEMINISM MEETS FERTILITY RITES
✳
May Day

The rains have stopped. The meadow that was brown and dry now wears bright spring green. See the wild irises? Who said purple and green do not go together? Everything seems to shout, "Come out, come out, wherever you are!" It is the first of May, celebrated since the dawn of agriculture for the rebirth of nature's fertility. This is the high point of the year, the moment when we weave ourselves and our dreams to a pole connecting earth and heaven in a glorious riot of color, movement, and music.

A hundred or so women and men gather annually in this meadow atop a hill where new grasses and wildflowers bloom, to dance around a gigantic carved Maypole decked with flowers in celebration of the marriage of Goddess and God. People come here from far and wide, considering themselves lucky to have received one of only a hundred invitations issued every year. Where else in the world are the ancient fertility mysteries still celebrated in their full glory? In these ancient and newly created rites, each year this community of Neopagans bind their lives to the miracle of regeneration through the sexual symbolism of planting the Maypole in the earth.

May Day, or Beltane, its Celtic name, is opposite Halloween on the calendar. Halloween marks a turning inward, a battening down of the hatches and going inside; May Day is the call to awaken. The earth is new again. If the year had only two seasons, Halloween would mark the beginning of winter, the time to pull in and conserve resources, while May Day would usher in the glorious abundance of summer. The time of scarcity is over; now it's time to party!

The new lambs are large enough to slaughter one for the traditional spring feast. There are edible weeds that have been growing all winter through the rains, dandelion greens, onions, and early potatoes. Scarcity gives way to plenty. It is time to celebrate the earth in all its gifts. It is not only the rams who are randy. Flowers burst into brazen color and open their genitalia to bees, calling out with their perfume, "Come to me. Am I not beautiful?" Couples go out walking together on velvet green fields. It is courting time. The Maypole ritual celebrates human sexuality as a part of life's glorious dance of Eros.

In the Celtic and Northern European tradition, dancing the Maypole at summer's onset is as central a rite as visiting the stations of the cross during Lent is in the Catholic tradition. Despite the heterosexual nature of the symbolism, and the pervasive oppressiveness of the institutionalization of heterosexuality within the culture at large, fertility symbolism remains central to springtime in any nature-based ritual and symbol system. How could it not be? The earth is in bloom. Cows are calving, and kids are cavorting through green pastures. Even in popular Christian culture, eggs and rabbits make an Easter appearance, competing for airtime with that old rugged cross.

The Maypole rite seemed an ideal opportunity for women to reclaim their sexuality through appropriating and redeeming the symbolic language of sexual joining inherent in the Maypole ceremony. This is what my partner and I set out to do in the spring of 1991, as priestess and priest of this community's May Day festivities.

* RITUAL DESCRIPTION *

The Maypole ritual which I shall describe occurred as part of a forty-eight-hour Beltane festival. It would be impossible to describe or comment here on everything that occurred in the larger event. Therefore I shall confine my comments to the climactic fertility rite, the Maypole ritual, giving just enough sense of the other events to provide a context.

May Day, or Beltane, was planned as a full weekend of festivities. In the past, different people had taken responsibility for planning and leading the various ritual events of the festival, resulting in a sort of liturgical potluck. As the event leaders, my partner and I wanted the entire forty-eight hours to flow as a single liturgical composition, and sought permission to design it as a coherent whole. Our approach was to have all the activities of the weekend build to the Maypole celebration. To prepare participants for the moment of ecstatic union, we designed a series of experiences and confrontations. This included five distinct ritual events, beginning with separate Friday-night sweat ceremonies for the men and women (purgation), games and other activities during the day on Saturday (orientation), a fire ritual on Saturday night (letting go of the old), and finally the Maypole dance on Sunday (calling in the new), followed by a roast lamb feast (communion). All of these were part of a single magical work. Consequently the phases may appear confusing and, in some cases, redundant. The Maypole ritual had most of the stages of a rite contained within its own boundaries, but because it was part of a larger rite, some were deemphasized or out of their usual order.

As is common in major social rites of passage, a series of ritual events can last several days or longer, each with its particular purpose in the liturgical whole. This occurs in Japanese rites of accession, Nubian wedding ceremonies, and all sorts of initiations into manhood or womanhood.

Purgation

We began on Friday night with a purgation ritual, by holding separate sweat-lodge purification ceremonies for the women and men. In each sweat there were four rounds of passing the rattle around the circle while it grew hotter with the addition of hot rocks and steam. Participants spoke in turn about their love for people of the other sex, the ways in which sexism and patriarchy had affected their lives and the lives of those they loved, and how they participated in it. Finally, when the heat was almost unbearable, each voiced her or his personal prayer and commitment to ending the cycle.

Reflections

Purification rites are a part of high holy days in most traditions. In the Jewish tradition there is the Day of Atonement before the New Book is written. Many people consider the entire Lenten season to be a purification in preparation for the resurrection. Certainly many people, especially in the Orthodox tradition, fast and pray between Good Friday and Easter morning. In the Islamic world there is the month of Ramadan, when believers fast every day from sunup to sundown to cleanse themselves. Many Native American tribes use a sweat-lodge ceremony as a purging of body and spirit.

The Neopagan framework has no such purification rite of its own. The closest thing this tradition has to confession or atonement is the cauldron of transformation (see chapter 3). Based on some problems in the years prior to this one, it was the leaders' belief that participants would need to be purified of sexism, grief, and despair to be ready to celebrate new life in our May Day dance.

After some discussion, we elected to use the sweat lodge as our confessional framework, in spite of legitimate concern about the appropriation of Native American and other indigenous traditions by white Americans as yet another form of cultural imperialism. The group did so on the grounds that many of our members had participated in such ceremonies in the past, and were familiar with the customs and proprieties. We were fortunate to have among our members people who had been trained and empowered by tribal people to lead the ceremony. The sweat lodge is a local custom in Northern California, having come from the original indigenous tribes here. We believed that we could use it respectfully, and in the spirit in which it was intended. Given that ours is a nature-based tradition, similar in many ways to the indigenous North American traditions, it seemed consonant with our symbol system, not an exotic custom that we had appropriated as a novelty.

Letting Go of the Old

Saturday night was an all-night fire ritual for burning away the last of winter's hardships. There had been plenty of suffering that winter. The U.S. government had killed one hundred thousand Iraqi men, women, and children and wreaked untold damage on sacred sites and remembrances of the ancient Goddess, not to mention massive ecological devastation, in the ancient "cradle of civilization." We incorporated a cathartic despair-to-empowerment format into our all-night ritual to allow people to mourn what had been done in our name as Americans.[1] Surely we could not enter a sacred union without purging ourselves of such grief and rage as many of us felt that year.

Gathering and Creating Sacred Space

By Sunday morning we were ready. It was time to begin the Maypole preparations. The men were responsible for preparing the pole, symbol of the male sexual organ; the women were responsible for readying the ritual site, the Maypole crown, and the gate through which the pole would pass when the men arrived. The site for the Maypole ritual is several hundred yards from the fire circle, where the previous night's ritual had taken place. A winding path leads over a small gully, across a little bridge, up some stone steps, arriving at a gate constructed of branches, which form an archway over the path. This is the yoni gate, signifying the entrance into the sacred circle of the Goddess's body. It is used only once yearly, for the May Day ritual.

Each May Day morning the women and girls spend hours decorating the gate with brightly colored ribbons, dozens of flowers that we've bought or picked, and bells set to tinkle when someone walks through the gate. The freshest, most beautiful flowers are reserved for the crown that tops the Maypole, from which long, colored ribbons hang.

Upon completing the festooning of crown and gate, the women and girls processed, singing, toward the site where the Maypole would be planted. We made a circle all together, with none above any other. An experienced priestess walked its outer perimeter three times clockwise, setting up a strong container with good boundaries to hold our love magic. Different women speaking extemporaneously invoked the traditional four directions (east, south, west, and north) with their corresponding elements: air heavy with musk and light with laughter; fires of passion; deep, compassionate waters, and solid earth, flesh of our flesh, to ground it all.

R e f l e c t i o n s

Magical tradition says that every circle is connected to every other circle that has ever been or ever will be, in a "world between the worlds," our way of describing our liminal space. The circle forms a crucible that we create with our thoughts and energy, in which we can reform reality. Therefore it is important that we cast it well.

A circle also allows full participation. Everyone can see everyone else. We are sisters, finding the Goddess in each other's eyes, not strangers facing an authority figure. Within the circle we are inside the turning earth, the wheel of the year, the egg, and the womb of the Mother. From here our intentions can more easily work the magic of transformation.

Evoking the Goddess

Because we hold the Goddess to be immanent, we can call forth her many faces in each of the women present. One woman at a time stepped into the center of the circle and spoke the name of a goddess who embodied the qualities she wished to bring to the circle: Quan Yin for compassion, Changing Woman for transformation, Aphrodite for erotic love. It took time. As Lesley Northup notes, "The giving of a sacred name is an ancient ritual element, now often used in women's spirituality."[2] We beat each name on the drum, and chanted it back to the woman who spoke it, appreciating her in her many faces, calling her as she has been called in many places.

R e f l e c t i o n s

Is this cultural appropriation? As women of predominantly white European and Semitic descent, should we be calling only on deities from the lands of our own ancestors? We do call on them. We call on Greek Demeter and Hebrew Asherah for abundance, on Irish Brigid to bless our crafts. But we are hybrids. Also, I worry about the effect of honoring the divine only in white-faced deities.

Where may we learn to see the sacred in faces different from our own, if we worship only the names and aspects of the Goddess emanating from our own cultural roots? What about the places where our own cultural roots are sadly lacking? Where do we learn the wisdom that other cultures have to teach? Where, if not in our religious practices, can we develop the deep respect for diversity that we white Westerners so desperately need?

Is it possible to honor other cultures' deities and customs in a manner that is respectful? In our love of the Goddess in her many faces, is it not possible that we might develop a deeper regard for the cultures out of which the various stories arise? I know that my compassion for the people and land of Iraq is far deeper because of my love for their ancient goddesses, whose pain I felt with the falling of each American bomb. If carried to its extreme, the argument against cultural appropriation would have to insist that men worship only male deities, in order not to be appropriative. I, for one, want a world in which men have a powerful relationship to female divinity. What I do not want is men thinking they have a right to define femininity or the Goddess for women. Appropriation occurs not when others use a form or symbol, but when they define it and bend it to their own ends, removing it from its context as if they were its owners. ❧

Purgation: Cleansing the Site

There was a deep hole for the Maypole already dug in the center of the circle from years past. Someone suggested that we clean out the energies that we did not want present in this year's festivities. Each woman dug into the hole with her hands, removing some dirt, and speaking aloud to the group what she wished to expel from sexual union: manipulation, coercion, distrust, exploitation, shame. When we finished the cleaning, someone else suggested we imagine what we wanted there instead. Another woman suggested that we needed moisture, so we watered the hole with laughter and delight.

Reflections

Purgation in preparation for the Maypole rite occurred at three levels, over three separate events that weekend. The first was the sweat lodge on Friday night, which focused on confronting participants with their own sexism. The second was the Saturday-night fire circle, which mourned and offered up our societal grief to Kali, the Indian goddess of destruction and death. Cleansing the site was the third purgative act, in which we purged the site of the Maypole of all abuses that had occurred there in previous years so that we would not incorporate them into our magic. We named the ways in which sexuality has been degraded and turned against women. By naming and clearing away what has been heaped on us by a misogynistic culture, women reclaim female sexuality as sacred, and even rejoice in it. The spontaneous addition of moisture indicates the women's appreciation of and commitment to their own pleasure. ✪

Evoking the God, Welcome, and Ingathering

At last the men arrived, carrying the Maypole. It takes about thirty men to carry the pole this distance. It is a twenty-foot-long pole, approximately a foot in diameter, cut from the trunk of a young fir tree. At its head is a three-foot-long unmistakable male organ hand-carved of oak. The men had worked together for over an hour to ready themselves for this moment. My partner and priest had instructed them in moving together sensitively and slowly, centering in their bodies, working with their breath. Each man and boy had handled the carved head, breathing his energy and love into it, and uttering a blessing for a new way of being sexually. This time when they arrived there was no rush at the gate. They were swaying in slow motion, meditatively, serenading us with a chant of love they had written.

The women ran to meet them. Very slowly, one by one, the men entered through the yoni gate. At the gate, by prearrangement, the men gave their drums to the women so that they could dance to the rhythm of the women's bodies. The women took the drums and responded with hugs, kisses, and suggestive gestures. The message was "We love you, we love your bodies and your sexuality, as we love our own. There is no need for coercion here. Here is love and trust. Eros lives." My heart leapt. All the work we had done for this moment had been worth it. We had created a basis for a heterosexual coupling that was truly joyous, gentle, passionate, and loving, with equal participation by women and men.

Reflections ✿

Naomi Wolf observes wisely, "There has been a feminist 'deconstruction' of masculinity, but very little reconstruction. Perhaps it is time to recognize that all cultures codify maleness and femaleness within sexual symbolism and that we can create a new world in which those categories need not be fixed or oppressive, but neither do they need to be dismissed or devalued. Something beautiful—a mostly benevolent manhood—was being symbolized. . . . Precious little feminist language in the last century and a half, let alone the last two decades, has done justice to this quality and what it means to so many women."[3] In this section of the ritual, women boldly celebrated maleness. In so doing they were reframing it as something that need not be threatening or oppressive to women, and therefore as an attribute that could be celebrated, rather than feared. In the same spirit the men respected the sacredness and the rhythm of the women's bodies.

The transfer of the drums to the women should be noted in this regard. This structural move gave the women control over the pace of the movement. All literature on sacred sexuality seems to point to the importance of men's sensitivity to women's timing and readiness for union. This act put the women in the driver's seat of determining when and how the symbolic phallus would enter their sacred space. ◗⌀

Empowering a Central Symbol

Together the women and men carried the pole into the circle. This was a change from previous years, when the men alone had carried and placed it, leaving the women in a position where they could only accept or protest the men's style and pace of entry. Then my partner and I signaled the others to lay it down. "No rush. Let's wait a moment," we teased. There was one more piece of magical business to attend to before weaving the power into the pattern of our ribbons. This was our prayer for the future, the central magic of the weekend, the planting of seeds that we would energize by our dance. We had brought a handful of the ashes of our grief from the previous night's fire. We placed them into the hole as compost to fertilize the hopes and dreams we would plant there.

Then the children stepped forward with the seeds of the future. Into the Maypole hole they placed clay seeds they had shaped and painted in their group the day before. Each child told us what her or his seed stood for: peace, freedom for all people, fair treatment for animals, a clean environment, chocolate. We added earth and straw, then slowly, very slowly, we began to raise the pole on top of the seeds. At one end a man and a woman stood together and placed the flower and ribbon crown on top. At the other end, my partner and I guided the pole into the ground, while everyone else held the pole and toned as one voice. It rose to its full, magnificent height, releasing a canopy of ribbons that fell to earth quivering with anticipation. We tamped down the earth to secure the pole, and passed out the ribbons to the women, who shared them with the men and the children. (This way the women maintained control of the action and the pace.)

R e f l e c t i o n s ❦◉

The putting down of the Maypole was the pivotal moment of the rite according to Mary Collins, who called it "a ritualized coitus interruptus . . . requiring participants to extend themselves into a future beyond the anticipated pleasure of the moment."[4] In other words, we are controlling the energies and postponing the moment's pleasure in the service of a future that holds promise and joy for women and children, as well as men.

Collins asserts that this ritual in its feminist reconstruction is no longer a fertility ritual, but an ecofeminist ritual reeducation that will be remembered in the bodies of the participants. She asks, "When does a reinterpreted reconstruction of a fertility ritual cease to be a fertility ritual, even when it draws upon traditional practices of such ritualizing? These are questions I pose within . . . [ritual theorist Catherine] Bell's argument that [a central feature of] ritual practice is [that it is] embedded in misrecognition of what is being done, and directed to producing or reconfiguring a vision of power in the world."[5] In this reconfigured vision, men lend their power to women's leadership and children's hopes, creating a new harmony and joy for the community. ❧

Exposition and Investment

The new May king and queen, chosen by competing in the previous day's May games, entered the center of the circle, where the outgoing king and queen invested them with the energy of God and Goddess for performing the sacred marriage and fructifying the fields. It has long been a custom to bind the king, but not the queen, to the Maypole. This custom supposedly evolved from an ancient Near Eastern tradition in which the king, in order to be invested with the power to rule, had to marry the Goddess through her priestess.[6] To be accepted, the king was required to pledge his life to the land, if necessary sacrificing his life to fertilize the earth and feed his people. As the new May king had Eros evoked in him, I as priestess spoke the intent of our ceremony. The king was pledging his power in service to the earth. We were, with his permission, binding him to the Maypole with our dance, signifying the binding of male power with ties of love and allurement to the earth and to relationship. In so doing we were also binding ourselves to him. Thus power should always be bound to love and relationship, as well as to the earth, which is the source of our life.

Reflection ❧

This section continues to image men's power bound to or framed by relationship, rather than operating by coercion. Here we see a new/old version of male leadership, the archetype of the servant king, whose power is bound and beholden to the community, tied to the feminine with bonds of Eros. ❧

Raising Power

The dance could now begin. Drums came out and began beating a slow, erotic rhythm. Moving in and out, we sang three chants, weaving in overlapping layers like the ribbons we held.

In and out, around and around the Maypole we danced. Our beautiful red-haired queen danced for her beloved, half clad, lifting her skirts as we sang. Time became eternity. The tunes changed. Out came flutes and recorders.

> Hull and tow, jolly rumballoe.
> We were up long before the day-o
> To welcome in the summer, to welcome in the May-o
> For summer is a-cumin' in, and winter's gone away-o.[7]

Other chants followed as people continued to dance. Eventually, king and pole were a single form beneath a weave of multicolored ribbons. We stopped winding and fell to the ground, sending all the prayerful, erotic energy we had raised back to the earth, where our prayers for the future were planted along with wishes for her healing. We stepped back from the pole. Someone offered a poem about unbinding Eros. Then the queen cut the binding cords from her beloved. Like wild horses, the young king and queen galloped off to consummate their union on a hillside where a white deer came to bless them. The rest of us remained in the circle to seal the magic we had made, to reopen the container, to thank the forces of earth, water, fire, and air that had graced our circle. We passed a chalice of good May wine and one of water, along with a plate of bread and cakes, spilling some upon the earth in libation. Then we retired to the hillside for feasting and loving.

R e f l e c t i o n s

It was done. Shame and violence lay defeated; Metis was no longer devoured by Zeus, and Europa had been liberated, along with Leda, from the clutches of predatory birds and patriarchal myth. The ancient rite of sacred marriage had been redeemed through the creation of a new mythic reality in which power and sexuality were bound to love, where men freely danced to women's rhythms, neither as captives nor as captors. For one brief ritual moment there had been a truce in the war of the sexes, and it was possible to see with certainty that the celebration of sexuality, even of heterosexuality and fertility, need not exploit women. It had not been achieved without effort. Maintaining it would not be easy. The group would need to exercise constant vigilance to prevent themselves from slipping back into the patterns of sexism, misogyny, and exploitation that surround us all daily. But we had opened a door. We had called people to attend to the daily abusive reality and to create and experience a new paradigm. ☙

* FEMINIST ANALYSIS *

The purpose in designing and executing the Maypole ritual described herein, and the other ritual pieces leading up to it, was to fundamentally alter the power relationship of male to female by altering the feeling tone of the ritual and the way in which we used the sexual symbols in it. We intended to remove all implications and aspects of the subordination of women from the celebration of Eros. This was no small task.

For the two or three years prior to the year of which I write, many of the women had been upset by the tone of the Maypole ritual. The men had rushed into the circle with the Maypole and, like adolescent boys in the backseats of cars, tried to jam it hastily into the ground, once even breaking the statue of Pan on the altar. (Upon discussing the matter later, a few men said that they could not help it, that the Maypole had "a life of its own"! Where have we heard this before?)

In the year prior to the one of which I now write, some of the women (and a few committed men) actually had to shout to stop what was tantamount to a ritual rape of the earth. This had left some of the participants badly shaken, feeling that their most sacred rite, and the body of the Goddess, had been violated. For those who believe that ritual is a prayer in which the symbolic pattern one wishes to set in motion is symbolically enacted, it was especially upsetting. My partner and I vowed that this would not happen again. If the rite was based in heterosexual symbolism, we would use it to construct a symbolic joining of female and male as free and equal partners in joyous loving.

We set about constructing a sequence of ritual events that would reframe and prepare the community for this most sacred moment of sexual and spiritual union, fully embodied and fully divine. To accomplish this we worked at three levels in the redevelopment of the ritual:

1. We raised consciousness among female and male participants about the nature and effects of sexism in their lives.
2. We reframed and prepared for the ritual with a more intentional sense of the sacred than had characterized the event in recent years.
3. We made mechanical changes within the ritual which would give the women more control, particularly in the transfer of the drums, the placing of the pole, and the handing out of the ribbons.

However problematic certain rites may be, if feminist ritualists wish to operate within any tradition, they must be prepared to critique, transform, and, at times, redeem their traditions' rites. I consider it the task of feminism to redeem sexuality, and especially female sexuality, from the degradations heaped upon it by the popular culture and patriarchal religion.

Did we succeed, then, in redeeming the fertility rite? I believe that to the extent possible we both upheld and transformed tradition. Still, one must ask: What does it mean for lesbian women to participate in a celebration in which the symbolism is so blatantly and exclusively heterosexual? One can also question the value of celebrating biological fertility in an overpopulated world. One could ask, given these concerns, whether the Maypole ritual is worthy of redemption, or whether it should be consigned to the scrap heap of rites best forgotten, along with fatted calves and infant sacrifice. This brings us to the larger question of whether Neopagan ritual is any more feminist, and any more empowering to women, than any other system of worship.

One of the most important aspects of Neopagan liturgy, which this ritual shows, is that it celebrates the sacred within the natural world and within all of us. It celebrates embodiment. My woman's body is understood to be sacred and whole-y in all my life phases. My life in the physical world need not be separated from the life of my soul. Being rooted in one's body is seen as a virtue, not a vice. Sexuality is celebrated as sacred, not only for its reproductive value, but as a source of pleasure and connection, which is itself given positive value. Most important to women is the value of having a female image of the divine, linking us to a legacy of thousands of years of Goddess worship and a time when women were revered for their power and wisdom. The healing effect of this on our self-worth, our sense of ourselves as having a primary rather than a derivative existence, is beyond words.

I wish I could say that the changes we made in this community's May Day ritual brought about a feminist conversion in the community at large. The truth is that the leaders took a lot of flak for bringing in such "heaviness." Some men and women were angry about the challenges and confrontations presented by a feminist critique. Some men complained at "being controlled by the women," at not being given free rein with the Maypole, and at being asked in the sweat ceremony to confront sexism that they did not believe themselves to be party to. Some women complained that we were creating division between the sexes by focusing too much on pain and abuse. There was general annoyance at having to deal with concerns that many people believed themselves beyond, as members of a counter-culture and a "liberated" religion with a female deity. This may be the biggest problem with Goddess-centered ritual: it can lull one into complacency because the sexism is more insidious than flagrant.

There has been increased sensitivity and directness surrounding issues of sexual abuse since that year. There has not been another ritual rape in the Maypole circle. While it may be a long time before the seeds of the future world grow to fullness, they have been planted. Best of all, they have been planted by the children, who witnessed a set of images that contradicted everything that the commercial manufacturers of sex had taught them. They saw adult women and men of all ages, shapes, and sexual persuasions celebrating playful, sacred, erotic love. They experienced the divine embodied in female and male imagery. They understood that for sacred union to take place, there must be deep mutual respect. They had the rare opportunity to experience a joyous union of heaven and earth, female and male, fully embodied and fully divine.

THE FESTIVAL OF FIRST FRUITS

※

Loaf Mass

Early August, hot and sticky. Nowadays one hardly notices except in brief interludes between one air-conditioned place and the next. Where there is no air conditioning, whole families follow the ocean breeze, when they can. The summer I spent in Erassos, on the island of Lesbos, the entire village moved the mile and a half down the hill and set up tents on the beaches during the hot weather. I recall a Florida childhood of pool parties and beach picnics, swimming lessons, and the blistering pink nose I always had on the first day of school. Memories linger of summers by the lake and sunburns, or long hot rides on the subway to Coney Island, bringing with them the smell of suntan oil mixed with salt.

Falling midway between the summer solstice and the autumnal equinox, the Festival of First Fruits heralds the end of summer, always too soon. Never mind that the days are still long enough for barbecues after work. You know now, as you did not know in those long-ago summers, that there is just enough time to bring in the sheaves before the darkness closes in and the frosts begin. It is Lammas.

Lammas. Loaf Mass. Celebration and offering of the first fruits of the grain harvest, an ancient custom of the Sumerians, the Celts, and the Hebrews: "Honor God with your substance and the first fruits of all your produce; then your barns will be filled with plenty, and your vats will be bursting with wine" (Proverbs 3:9–10). The grain harvest was a big deal. Grain cultivation and storage was what allowed for the building of civilization as we know it.

Few people I know bake anymore. Nor do most of us look out our windows and see wheat ripening on sunlit hillsides. We see traffic, and we buy our bread at Safeway, or at Whole Foods. Nevertheless there is a common harvest from which we gather our fruits, at least those of us who live in a part of the world where food is relatively, if artificially, abundant. That is the harvest of the food that fills our table, planted every year by farmworkers, and grown courtesy of sun and earth. Built on that harvest is another harvest, the harvest of the first fruits that each of us has planted in our lives.

We do not have to look far, only as far back as the recent midwestern floods or this year's El Niño, to realize that we are still at the mercy of nature for all that we have. We are reminded of this when fisheries fail due to runoff from clear-cutting the forests, which puts silt into the streams. We remember this when we hear about the unexpected frost ruining the orange crop in Florida or the wine crop in the Napa Valley. In Northern California at this time of year we worry about fires burning out of control, taking everything we have given our precious lives to. It is as true today as it was five thousand years in our past: too much rain will rot the grain, too much sun will burn it.

People are still at nature's mercy. This offends the human sense of mastery. We want to rise up shouting, "I am the captain of my ship, I am the master of my fate." We live in an advanced technological society five thousand years past Sumer. We have farming methods that operate like fertility drugs, extracting growth from land that is exhausted. We could almost believe that our food is not dependent on nature's mercy. But until we can eat virtual food, we will depend on earth and sun to create the miracle of photosynthesis, which grows our food. Our existence will continue to depend upon forces beyond our control.

Forces, not things. People used to refer to those forces by name. They called them Sekhmet, for the fierce Egyptian sun personified as a lioness, or Hapi, the river that would overflow its banks every year fertilizing the entire Nile Valley. (Now they have dammed the river, and the Nile Valley is no longer fertile.) Later these forces came to be known as gods, but the gods still embodied the forces of nature. Inanna was the fertile fields of earth and the storehouse filled with grain. Even as they built their city-states, the Sumerians knew that without Inanna, there was no civilization. For this reason they would hold an elaborate ritual marriage of their king to the Goddess each year, as described in the previous chapter. This ensured that the forces of fertility would be on their side. The entire ancient world depended upon the grain harvest ripening in the storehouses, which would keep the people through the winter.[1]

* RITUAL DESCRIPTION *

These forces, whatever we call them, sustain or destroy life today. We can pretend that there is no life in these forces of nature. Engineers lull us into thinking we can reduce them to their chemical elements and control them with dams, levees, and artificial fertilizers. When all is said and done they remain. The sun. The rain. The fertility of the topsoil. The river that overflows, taking houses foolishly built in the wake of levees we thought would last. By whatever name, this is the power that people propitiated or honored at Lammas—the Great Without Whom Nothing, on whose mercies their lives depended. That was the bottom-line name for all the gods. The rest is just commentary.

Something seems to be missing in our relationship to that greater power. As our abundance increases, our gratitude seems to diminish. Perhaps it is the very absence of this give-back mentality that has us thoughtlessly raping and strip-mining the earth, importing foods from people who are starving, using farming methods that do not return nutrients to the soil, and fishing practices that are depleting even the vast oceans, and glutting ourselves on food and drink that are killing us. We no longer honor the Great Without Whom Nothing. And soon we may be left with nothing.

Am I suggesting that we should propitiate some rain god, or slaughter the first-born calf on the altar of Baal? Not exactly. I am suggesting we arrange a ceremonial lull in our busy everydayness to remember the forces of nature that sustain us, and to give back to them. I am suggesting we make a place in our liturgical calendar for recognizing that our abundance does not belong to us alone, that it comes only with the blessing of the Great Without Whom Nothing, the one we call Mother Nature.

What would such an honoring look like? It used to look like a harvest festival at which a sheaf of grain or the first loaf of bread from the season's harvest was offered to the reigning deity: "You must also bring a sheaf of the first fruits of your harvest to the priest" (Leviticus 23:10). The people offered their first and their best, not their leftovers, hoping to gain favor for the remainder of the harvest. (Remember Cain and Abel? See Genesis 4:1–7.) We might make an offering, even what one might call a sacrifice, in thanksgiving for the first fruits of our harvest. Lammas rites include both a celebration and a sacrifice.

In some traditions families make a large gift to their temple or to their tribe when they have good fortune. In other traditions, people tithe all income. These are offerings made in gratitude to the forces that bestow fortune, the Great Without Whom Nothing.

In today's world, most of us are not in the habit of making large gifts. When we give outside our families it is usually what is left after we have helped ourselves. That is considered normal, even good sense. But there is a price for our selfishness, paid in alienation and a sense of helplessness about our world. We reap a harvest of our isolation and hubris.

I consider Lammas a time to make a gift that may pinch a little, in thanksgiving for the first fruits of my abundance. One year I gave to my church. Another year I gave to an organization that preserves a forest sanctuary of uncut redwoods. The year I shall tell about now is the year in which a group of friends and an independent art gallery created a ritual rock concert in Golden Gate Park to benefit the Institute for Food and Development Policy, also known as Food First.

Food First works for both the end of human starvation and the preservation of the earth by promoting sustainable farming practices in developing countries. Giving to them gives back to the earth and to the people in developing countries whose harvest we too often place on our own tables. We began to set the wheels in motion for the first annual San Francisco Festival of First Fruits.

If we wish to reintroduce ancient customs and symbols into present-day culture, we must do so in a style that people can relate to in the present. Most modern people cannot relate to robed Druids chanting arcane incantations on a sunny afternoon in the park, except as a curiosity. A free outdoor concert, on the other hand, is an accepted form of summer celebration in late-twentieth-century city life. The whole event could be a Lammas celebration, a modern Festival of First Fruits. The plan was to embed a sacred space and ritual order in the fabric of a rock concert, and inseparable from it. It would simply be a matter of pushing the boundaries of the form to turn it into a sacred celebration and offering. We could weave the ritual elements into and throughout the music, leading up to a request for people to participate in making offerings to Food First.

Setting Up and Defining a Central Symbol

We reserved the band shell and secured a sound permit. We would claim the whole grassy area around the band shell as sacred space. We conceived of a way to define a permeable circle, with color and sound, so that passersby could move into and out of the ritual space at will. Using red, gold, and white banners at each entrance, across the back of the band shell, and on the lip in front, to symbolize the high heat of summer, we erected a huge altar of first fruits on the apron of the main stage. The central image on the altar was a life-sized golden goddess sculpture kneeling, raising her arms above her head, as in a gesture of receiving grace and spilling over with abundance. Over her arms were draped strings of beads and scarves of gold. Surrounding her were plants, flowers, summer greenery, and huge baskets of fruits. A specially baked loaf of barley raisin bread was placed before her. This imagery bespoke the graciousness and abundance we wished to evoke, embodying nature's continuous flow of giving and receiving. Consistent with that imagery, we placed large papier mache urns on columns at each entrance where a masked drummer was to be stationed. However, as we did not circulate information on Food First, or on the purpose of the event, the urns, intended for donations, did not get much action.

We also attempted to create a circle of sound. The idea was to station masked drummers dressed in red shirts at each of the entrances to the area, so that people would enter into a circle of rhythm. Continuous drumming would commence at the opening of the festival and continue to the end, climaxing during a power-raising ceremony of offering. Without being told, people wandering through the park would know by visual and auditory cues that they were crossing a magical line. For so long as they remained within the area bordered by the drummers, this magical rhythm would surround and move through them. Instead of words, a central, ever changing beat would define the space and act as the foundation of our event.

This took some technical planning. To keep all the drummers holding the circle in synch with each other, we would need to put speaker monitors around the circle amplifying a rotating master drummer, who would set a rhythm from the stage. The master drummer would not be heard on the stage, in order not to interfere with the band, but only from the speakers defining the circle. Furthermore, the master drummer would have to take rhythmic cues from the band, and use that to set a steady beat that continued between songs. We needed several good ritual drummers who could listen, then set and hold a rhythm without showboating or making themselves the center of attention.

R e f l e c t i o n s

The circle of sound was the pivotal detail that defined this ritual as a ritual. There can be no ritual except inside a space that is in some way distinguished from the rest of the world and claimed as sacred. For such a loosely knit rock concert in the part to work as a ritual, we needed enough competent drummers to hold the circle in a contained space. There is no magic without a container, and in this case the container would be primarily auditory.

Sometimes one tries things that don't work. I like pushing edges. In this case, it was critical not only to recruit a large number of drummers (conga, dumbek, djembe, even Taiko), but also to train them in their role. Their job was to hold the sacred space with sound. It was important that they work together as a team, even to the point of being dressed in an identifiable way. Otherwise, while there might be good drumming, there would be no ritual container. I requested gold masks and headbands for them to wear.

This is where the plan broke down. Perhaps people simply had too much to do. The person in charge of recruiting the drummers had too many other tasks. Perhaps he let this one slip. Perhaps my partner and I had not adequately communicated the pivotal nature of this detail. A musician and promoter not experienced in the fine points of ritual probably did not fully grasp its centrality. Perhaps we had devised too elaborate a plan for the team of volunteers executing it. I don't know. Probably all of these were factors. For whatever reason, we did not have a corps of drummers holding the space. There were too few drummers to do the job, and they wandered in and out at will. In the end there was no ritual container. As a result the event, which had been conceived as an experimental synthesis of rock concert and ritual, only worked as a good rock concert with a theme, not as a ritual. It was an interesting experiment, which is why I tell it here.

Gathering and Creating Sacred Space

The day began, as do many such events, dealing with breakdowns. The fellow with the drummers' costumes and the fabric drapes had not shown up yet (which was okay, as neither had most of the drummers). Someone else was coming with the fruit for the altar, but no one could remember who that was. The drummers who were scheduled to perform from the Taiko group had not been asked to also be ritual drummers to hold the space. Worse, they seemed unaware that there was a second time during the concert when they would be drumming, toward the end of the show, to raise energy for the offering. Many of them had planned to perform and leave. I tried to talk them into staying.

As all this was going on, six different bands were setting up their equipment on the stage. The sponsoring organization had hired a professional stage manager who was truly a Goddess-send. He soothed ruffled feathers and kept everything running on time. He was a genius at supervising the smooth switching of bands and the running of sound, either of which, done poorly, can ruin a performance of any sort.

Our sound permit began at noon and ended at exactly 5 P.M. We had to start on time to get everything in. At 11:55 the Taiko drummers opened the event with a ritual prayer in Japanese calling for the dragon to fly over the fields and turn the energy from sad to happy. The drummers dancing around the drums in formation and shouting accompanied the loud beating of big drums. It is a powerful way to open a ritual. It gets everyone's attention and focuses the energy. In Wiccan terms, it functions as a banishing by clearing the air with its loudness and the power of its intention, so that there is room to put something else in the space. Having opened the space, we could cast a circle. The first master drummer took his position unobtrusively at the rear stage-left microphone, and the sound system went on.

Without a word of introduction, my partner and I took the stage. Standing close to the audience in front of the band area, Rick asserted the beat on his dumbek. The first master drummer followed, setting a rhythm for the drummers at the edges of the circle. A circle of sound began. We sang, "We are a circle within a circle, with no beginning and never ending," encouraging everyone to sing the chorus with us. The verses of this song, sung by circling groups around the world, call on the four elements within and around us. The final verse seals the circle: "The circle closes between the worlds to mark this sacred space where we come face to face."[2]

The heartbeat continued as solo vocalist Chris Berkner came to the microphone. With a voice like an angel, he sang an unaccompanied invocation to the spirit of life, calling on the Great Without Whom Nothing to be present for our rites, to accept our offerings. The drum followed his lead.

Welcome and Exposition

Then and only then was it time to welcome the audience to the festival. The drumming continued in the background as I welcomed people to the event and stated our purpose for the day. We used this opportunity to introduce the sponsor and founder of the event, who in turn introduced the speaker from Food First, our beneficiary.

Reflections

After the circle is cast and the directions are called is generally a good point at which to perform introductions and expositions. It is generally wise to start a ritual on a mid-high-energy note, to focus the attention. Then, if necessary, follow with exposition. Exposition lowers the energy level. Before doing it, it is important to get people present in the space. After the circle is cast, and people are in it, welcome and exposition are possible from a place of relatedness. I shared a little about first fruits in our lives and in nature, and invited all present to share in celebrating and offering them. There are always people to thank in a volunteer event, and it is important to do so graciously. One does not, however, want to interrupt the energy once the ritual starts building to a climax. Acknowledgments and announcements definitely fall into the area of foreplay and generally should happen early in the ritual.

Invoking

Having introduced ourselves and welcomed the audience, it was time to welcome our guests of honor, the earth and the sun, our Great Without Whom Nothing. It was also time to start the show. Rick and I took the stage again, this time with other musicians on keyboard, drums, electric violin, bass, and guitar backing us up. The first song was to invoke the Sun God. Rick began to sing as the violinist played a haunting descant line.

> We sing an anthem to the Sun,
> As you reach your peak of power,
> Ever shorter days become,
> But like the tides your light must flow and ebb until the cycle's done.[3]

Immediately after this song, the drummer began a heartbeat rhythm. I took the mike and invited the audience to join us in the chant that formed the backup blues line of our invocation to the Goddess. "She's a dance away, she's a rollin', she's a rollin'." I kept repeating it, taking my microphone out into the audience, until others began to join in. A few got up to dance, as Rick began the first verse. We were singing the dance of the earth, the dance of life, the dance of nature, celebrating our part in it. I joined him in the chorus:

> You've got to dance, dance, dance, just like your Mama does.
> She's sayin' dance, dance, dance, c'mon dance with me.[4]

The band faded out. All that remained was the heartbeat behind the voices of the audience and priestess invoking the Goddess. By the end many people were out of their seats dancing in front of the stage. The celebration had begun.

Reflections

A word about invoking the Goddess in mixed public rituals: just do it! If there is nothing hokey or self-conscious about the invocation, and it is done with a simple metaphor like Mother Nature (her most common name), no one is likely to object. In this case we were speaking of the Goddess poetically as the generative force of life. Generative is by biological definition female, that is, able to generate new life. Male seems to be nature's wild card. Male force, like the sun, is the biological catalyst that disrupts the equilibrium in the generative force, causing transformation, insemination, splitting. This is how sperm inseminates egg. Note that the egg and the earth are generative, not inert. One can use the same metaphor in considering the bolt of lightning that sparked life in earth's primordial soup. The joining of earth and sun allows for the growth of life and vegetation that permit us to live on this planet.

Still, it is a metaphor. In the end what we address is not a man or a woman in the great beyond but a force beyond all our metaphors, which at best gives us a useful map for approaching the territory of the ineffable. It is valuable to remember that a metaphor is never right or wrong; it is simply useful or not useful. We do not wish to reify the divine female in an image of the earth and darkness, nor the male as the god of sun and light. According to de Beauvoir, it was just this identification of female with the seemingly passive earth, and the male with the active seed, that went hand in hand with the loss of status for women as agriculture developed. Moreover, not every pantheon has a female earth goddess and a male sun god. Egyptians honored their fierce sun as goddess. So did the Celts, in their worship of the goddess Brigde. These metaphors fit with the cycles of nature and life, as they understood them.[5]

Raising Energy

To return to the concert, by now we had created sacred space, gotten everyone present through welcoming, acknowledging, and introducing the day and its purpose, and called in the forces we wished to honor. Now we started to turn up the heat. We began with a solo artist singing with acoustic guitar, and increased the power of each subsequent offering until we arrived at the band with top billing, who were wild and fun, and sure to get everyone dancing. Meanwhile life was proceeding offstage.

Offstage events had not been as well organized as the onstage part of the event. The organizers had a vision of many booths filled with art, crafts, organic food, and nonprofit groups doing good work. Alas, too few volunteers doing too much work prevented the sponsoring group from enrolling the number of businesses and organizations needed to create the fairground atmosphere envisioned. There were a few artists, and a few food booths. Some people sat on the grass enjoying picnics. Others came and went. It was a pleasant enough summer day.

Drummers drifted in and out of formation at the entrances, and the urns were forgotten or ignored. Rick did manage to maintain a central rhythm by rotating master drummers through the position on stage, but without the physical presence of masked, costumed drummers at the entrances and exits holding the energy in, I am not sure it made much of an impact.

The Work: Offering and Committing Ourselves

The concert was a success. The bands were great, and built nicely to the climax of the offering. Following the final rousing set by Noah's Great Rainbow, I took the stage while a straggly band of drummers set a beat in the background (the Taiko group had long since left). I began to invite people, in a rhythmic guided imagery, to recall the journey of the seed, and to remember the seeds they had planted in their lives that past spring, or the ones that had germinated underground through the winter, which were now beginning to bear fruit.

"Take a moment now," I said. "Tune into your own body. Notice the sense of ripening you feel as the earth's fruits ripen. Feel your body. Take a deep breath and notice how it has opened since winter. Notice how ripe and juicy you feel? This is the time of ripening. Look around your life. You have a harvest, even if you are not a gardener. What is there that was not there before? What has grown, fruited, ripened in your life this summer? What is growing and ripening right now? Look around and notice the friendships, the projects, and the ideas that may be ripening in the summer sun, turning golden. Is it not a wonder how those little seeds have grown? Are these not miracles? Consider the richness these new fruits will bring into your life in the coming winter. Consider your gratitude. How will you say 'Thank you' to the growing force in life? What would you like to offer? In ancient times, people offered their first fruits each season on the altar, in thanks for their blessings—their first and their best. What are your first fruits? What will you give back in gratitude and prayer for an abundant harvest?"

The intensity of the drums increased. I took out my offering, a check just a little more than I would normally give, written to Food First, and waved it. "Here is my offering. I am offering $100 in thanks for my first fruits. This is in thanks for the first investments in a new project. Who will join me?" I invited people to come forward with offerings. Baskets and urns went out among the crowd to collect Lammas gifts for Food First.

As the urns were returned, the same solo vocalist who had called on the spirit of life early in the concert came to the front and again improvised a song/chant of offering. His voice rang out as the drums blended softly in the background. Then a speaker from New College came forward and gave a brief, pointed homily regarding giving and community, speaking to what we had done inside the power of community, and what remained to do in our world. The drums continued behind him, giving his words extra power.

Reflections

How ready we are to spend $50 or $100 on a pair of shoes, a massage, a workshop, or a restaurant meal! Women actively encourage one another to do so. When a friend tells me she has purchased something for herself, I am likely to respond, "Good for you!" The prevailing feminist ethic says that women have given too much for too long. We should place ourselves first, take care of ourselves, should even be selfish. Yet ask most of us for a contribution to something we believe in, something that will make the world a better place for ourselves, our children, our sisters, and we will tell you we cannot afford it. We will offer $5 or $10, maybe $25 on a good week. I am guilty of this myself. We have a tendency, like Cain, to offer the leftovers, what we think we can spare after we have taken care of our own and our families' needs and wants, not merely the basic necessities.

Such a contribution is not an offering. I would assert, further, that this attitude toward giving is not in our interest as feminists. It perpetuates a patriarchal system of rugged individualism in which we are each in the world alone, to satisfy our own needs independent of, or in competition with, the needs of others. It is a fundamental principle of feminism that our solutions are not individual. As women we know that our needs are not separate from the needs of those around us. Nor are our resources best used by hoarding them. We are best served through the interdependent sharing of tools and resources. Feminist scholar

Clare Fischer calls this the lactation model, in which the more we give, the more there is available to give.

Feminists are committed to a vision of the world in which there is harmony and sufficiency for all. According to Genevieve Vaughan's feminist criticism of exchange, *For-Giving,* giving is the basis of feminist economics.[6] I would assert that giving out of a sense of abundance is a feminist act, breaking up the patriarchal paradigm of scarcity. There is enough to share. The offering of first fruits may be a pre-patriarchal custom going back to the days of women's social and religious leadership.

This is what we attempted to model in our Lammas rite. It was a beginning. If the founding organization were to build on what we did, in a few years we would have the beginnings of a new old tradition. It would take a shared understanding of purpose, alignment on goals and methods, and sufficient time and volunteers to do a major publicity campaign in which all spokespeople would talk about the offering aspects of the event. We could start a San Francisco custom, an annual first fruits festival of giving. We could invite a number of earth-focused nonprofits to participate. People would arrive eager to give. Perhaps they would walk from table to table looking at literature, deciding where this year's Lammas gift should go. For this first event, we had not given people adequate preparation. They did not write checks. Instead they did the usual rummaging for "spare" change and bills. When the urns came back to the stage, they were not nearly as full as we had hoped. ✪

Completion

As the final speaker was concluding his remarks, Rick began the keyboard introduction to the final song, as is often done at the close of a sermon in African American Christian churches to create a segue between sermon and hymn. The benediction put a cap on the day, sending people out with a sense of blessing and spreading the energy we had invoked. Rick and I wrote "Never You Fall" as an earth benediction. It calls on the forces of earth, air, fire, and water to bless the congregants as they leave. Just as "We Are a Circle" is one of my favorite ways to cast a circle, "Never You Fall" is a favorite way to take one down, especially in large public groups. The first verse takes down the circle, leaving us in the great web of life, and calls on earth to continue to guide us as the ground of our being. Then it reminds us to be called by a vision of liberation:

> May the Web of Life weave its pattern all around you,
> May the ground of being guide your feet,
> May the grand design of liberation, liberation be your call,
> Never you fall, never you fall.[7]

As this gentle song is coming to an end, the beat picks up in a surprising move. It pulls forward like a band of horses eager to break their reins and run away. To an alternating 5/4 and 7/4 beat, we sent the audience forth on a wave of high energy, charged to go out and "turn the world around." The ritual was complete. The stage manager turned off the sound right on time, and the bands began packing up their gear.

✳ FEMINIST ANALYSIS ✳

What had we done here? Was it ritual? Was it feminist? If the art is bad, it is unlikely that the ritual is good. But if the art is good, does that mean anything about the ritual? Was it feminist? Putting forth a female image of the divine in a large public gathering is certainly an act that empowers and emancipates women. It was not, however, "the production of the community of worshipers," a principle that Collins considers basic to feminist liturgy. That is, the community did not create it in the act of participation. It was created from the stage rather than in the interaction between the stage and the crowd, as I would have wished. Had the ritual events offstage been emphasized more, the balance might have shifted. On other counts, it passed Collins's feminist muster. It certainly produced an event that was in no way text based, and the ritual aspects of the event developed a "distinctive repertoire of ritual symbols and strategies."[8] Ron Grimes discusses what he terms "ritual infelicity," which sounds like a good label for what went wrong that day.[9] What was missing? What, had it been present, would have made the crucial difference? One is never sure, but I would guess that the answer lies in the areas of organization and enrollment.

Because of other commitments I had not taken much responsibility for the recruiting and organizing of volunteers. In the end there were too few harried volunteers, too much to do, too little time in which to do it, differing priorities, and insufficient understanding about what I regarded as key ritual components and what it would take to accomplish them. Pieces fell through the cracks, and the ritual focus got lost. Had I, or someone working with me who was fully cognizant of how all the pieces needed to work together, organized and managed the ritual part of the event, there would have been more attention to certain details, and this would have better secured its workings as a ritual.

Drummers would have been found and invited into the planning process earlier, not added at the last minute. They would have understood the centrality of their role. Costumes would have been procured and tried out for workability ahead of time. Drummers would have been coordinated with the clown who, without proper instruction, wandered around aimlessly. There would have been advance publicity about a festival of giving, and more emphasis on filling the urns with offerings from the crowd. In other words, the offstage parts of the ritual would have been as coordinated and rehearsed as what was happening on stage.

This would have been a change from what is usual and familiar in putting on a concert, so it fell by the wayside, as the unfamiliar is likely to do without sufficient alignment and emphasis.

I have learned that it is virtually impossible to both serve as priestess and manage an event. They require two different states of consciousness, one very open and receiving, the other managerial, left-brained, and task focused. I believe that in all rituals of more than eight or ten people the priestess should have a co-leader who functions much like a good stage manager. The priestess should not be expected to find and train volunteers, to work with a group on design (which means organizing and facilitating meetings), to acquire whatever is needed to set up and decorate the ritual space, to preside at the rite, and then to clean up afterward. This is not what we would expect from a man in the same position.

There is something here to be examined, having to do with what we women expect from one another and from ourselves. After another ritual, exhausted from the work of planning, setting up an elaborate room, and presiding at two initiations, I found myself at day's end on the floor ironing spilled wax out of the rug. A colleague asserted that something was wrong with this picture. "Can you imagine a priest having to iron the wax out of the carpet after saying mass?" she asked. No, I could not. But I had always opposed the hierarchy and elitism of the Roman priesthood. Was my doing the cleanup not evidence of a sisterhood of equality?

If so, where were my sisters? They apparently did not feel equally responsible for restoring the room to order. Feminists need to keep a vigilant eye out for a tendency to overwork and burn out women leaders. In the name of equality we can oppress our leaders, turning them into overworked mothers of the community. After all, Mom is often the only and certainly the earliest model most of us have of female power. The way our culture treats mothers provides the model for our expectations, resentments, and overall treatment of female leadership. Generally the way we treat mothers is to love them only so long as they are serving and nurturing, expecting the fount of giving to be never-ending. When at last it dries up from one too many sinks full of dishes after a full day of work and mothering, we are irate. We respond like three-year-olds. Not surprisingly, this is the way we treat our priestesses and other female community leaders. Worse, this is the way we treat ourselves.

I am left with looming questions about how to apply democratic, feminist principles to organizing and running a large event. How do we empower expertise without setting up hierarchy? How do we promote equality without burning out leaders? How do we empower leadership without authoritarianism? These are not easy questions, but they are the questions with which we must grapple if feminist values and forms are to make a difference in the larger world.

As we are examining the ritual's failures, let us turn once again to the question of the ritual's thematic purpose: the offering of first fruits. Tom Driver, in *The Magic of Ritual*, writes at length about the use of ritual to establish moral and social order.[10] As feminists seeking to alter the value system of our culture, we can use ceremonial occasions as the opportunity to set new standards of normative behavior. If we do not make use of ritual to create and assert feminist values, we may be merely entertaining ourselves in feel-good circles. Feminist ritual is not just about empowering ourselves as individuals inside a patriarchal context. It is about fundamentally altering, through ritual actions and symbols, the power relationships and values that have kept women and nature in a subordinate position. One way of tying these ritual actions to the outside world is to empower them through funding our values, making offerings to what we love and to visions that call us.

What, besides presenting a concert on a sunny afternoon in the park, did we accomplish? If religion does not live in the world, whom and what does it serve? If one is not making a difference, is this the best use of time and effort? Had there been any education about giving? Had there been an occurrence of the sacred, an honoring of the Great Without Whom Nothing?

Certainly providing people with a way to celebrate the season by holding a free day of entertainment in a sunny park in the city is a worthwhile effort. For some members of the organizing group, that was plenty! One could say that the music itself was an offering, and it would be true. People enjoyed themselves, the music was good, and the event worked as an aesthetic whole. Perhaps a little money was raised for Food First. But I am left wondering, did it make a difference in the world? Did it serve the Great Without Whom Nothing?

This is always my question, as an activist using ritual as my primary tool for transformation. Sacred seasonal rituals have traditionally been used to rebind human lives to the cycles of nature, to move people to pause and consider from whence their lives and blessings come, and to touch more deeply into the love that binds all life together.

Perhaps it is love that is the key to the giving I had hoped to inspire. When we are in love, nothing can stop us from bestowing gifts upon our beloved. Clearly some work of love is present in the universe. That love is pouring out her gifts upon us all the time. Feel her breathing fresh air into our lungs from her tree body. Smell her fruits and flowers. She is giving and producing constantly. Mostly we take her gifts for granted. We can give back to her, thank her for her love, by giving to restore the earth's balance and harmony. Perhaps where the rite failed was in getting people in touch with her love flowing over us, and our love for her in return. Perhaps had that occurred the material gifts would have been automatic.

THE SEVEN-GATED PASSAGE

✳

The Autumnal Equinox

Fall brings crispness to the air in New York. Not so in Northern California, where September is the hottest month of summer. Those extra days of warm sunshine can nearly lull us into an illusion of endless summer. Then the autumnal equinox creeps up, taking us just a little by surprise. Could it be here already? Yes, summer is over, the air whispers, and almost immediately turns cooler, as if to say, did you think you could play forever?

Autumn is the reckoning. Grain harvest brings feast or famine. Now comes the ingathering, the time to harvest what was planted. Whatever is not gathered and stored in time will rot or go to seed. Suddenly everyone is busy with old and new projects. People become like little squirrels, storing nuts for winter. What's done is done. Now make the most of it.

Autumn calls for the scythe. It is time to learn limits. Cut away the fat. Cull the herd. Agrarian people face the tough question of which animals will make it through the winter. What lives and what dies? The question arises in a different context as people living rushed urban lives survey their calendars with alarm. What stays, and what goes? Advertising to the contrary, perhaps it is not possible to have it all. Autumn is a reminder that some things must be left behind. In the fall, trees shed their leaves. People get rid of extra baggage they cannot carry into the next season of life. Perhaps one can postpone the decision until Halloween, when the chill sets in, but sooner or later choices must be made.

✳ RITUAL DESCRIPTION ✳

Unlike most autumn rituals, which celebrate harvest, this is a ritual of cutting. The ritual event described here fell halfway between the autumnal equinox and Halloween—a good time for a rite of passage. Designed and performed for an annual conference called the Dance of Change, put on by the feminist spirituality master's program at Immaculate Heart College Center, it draws on the archetypal imagery of the seven gates of initiation, which strip down the initiate in preparation for spiritual rebirth. The conference theme was "Spirituality, Political Power, and Imagination." The program notes read, "If women are to take political power we will have to invent a future for ourselves that is not based in our past, but is embodied in our spirit. To do this we must use our collective imagination. In this ritual workshop we shall enter the unknown, creating a future of power."

When a person carries an old way of thinking and being into a new life, the new life begins to bear an uncanny resemblance to the old one. The male-dominated and male-defined world is like the water a fish swims in, invisible and pervasive. It defines human existence and assumptions about "the way things are." How is it possible to design a future of power and spirit for women that does not arise out of the water of women's subordinated past? If feminists want a future that does not look like the past, it will require shedding old ways of being. A line from a Robin Morgan poem in the early seventies prophesied, "We must risk unlearning what has kept us alive."[1] How?

Initiations provide a framework for leaving the past behind and taking on a way of being that is more appropriate to one's new life. By cutting the cord to the past, rites of passage ease the initiate across the boundary to the unknown.[2] The conference planners wished to empower women to actively imagine and design a future that radically breaks with the structures of patriarchy. In casting aside subjugated ways, women might design a future actually based in women's power, spirit, and imaginations. The following feminist rite ushered a small group of women from the patriarchal past into living and standing for a feminist future.

Creating Sacred Space

The conference was being held in a school building belonging to the religious community hosting the event. The planning committee assigned our workshop to a large classroom full of desks and blackboards, complete with math posters on the wall. It was cheery and institutional, just the sort of atmosphere one would not want for a liminal rite. If we were to create an authentic rite of passage, we would have to thoroughly alter the environment to make it unrecognizable as a classroom, or as anything else the initiates had ever seen.

A rite of passage alters consciousness through the juxtaposition of familiarity and surprise.[3] The site itself was the element of familiarity. The first surprise was the way in which we transformed the setting. We wanted to shock awake anyone expecting to enter an ordinary conference workshop. Instead initiates entered a sacred space as dark and blank as a shroud, empty of any worldly signs from their past. We set to work on the afternoon before the ritual, with help from the custodial staff. It took two of us approximately six hours just to prepare the room. We covered every wall and blackboard with white sheets. Heavy curtains closed out the light from the bright Southern California day. Around the perimeter of the room we placed large white candles in clear glass jars, providing our only light. By nine o'clock that evening we had transformed the classroom into a passageway that led through the liminal zone of the underworld, into a blank space where we could write our future.

Defining a Central Symbol

In the center of the left wall as one entered the room was a drape of white gauze, extending out from the wall, then draping four feet across the ceiling, until it fell from the ceiling to the floor. This was the gate through which initiates would be required to pass seven times on their journey. The gate was mysterious, ominous. It was the white of blank paper, on which everything is yet to be written. Making it of gauze conjured veils that must be shed or passed through on the way to spiritual power.

R e f l e c t i o n s

The veil or gate between dimensions and domains of reality was the central symbol for this initiatory rite. The gate is a symbol for passage, crossing over, piercing through.[4] It is the limen, the threshold between here and there, standing in the null zone of neither. It stood for the passage that women must make to create a feminist future born of our collective imagination. The women were to pass through the gate, pierce the veil seven times, sacrificing something each time, at last arriving in a place where they could envision a future from nothing.

We did not choose the number seven arbitrarily. Seven has mystical significance in nearly every tradition. There are seven days in a week. Rumi speaks of seven stages to initiation. We have seven chakras, seven sacraments. We have all heard of the Dance of the Seven Veils. There is also an ancient Sumerian tale of the Goddess's descent to the underworld, in which she must pass through seven gates, shedding something of herself at each gate, before being resurrected.[5] This was our model for the ritual.

Gathering

Ye Ye Ife, a gifted feminist ritualist and priestess of Oshun from San Diego, trained in the Yoruba tradition, designed and priestessed the ritual with me. She was the guide and I was the gatekeeper. She awaited the participants in the hall outside the classroom while I made the final preparations in the room, lighting candles and burning sage to purify the space. Ye Ye Ife was covered in a veil of the same gauze as the gate, giving her an otherworldly appearance. As the women arrived, talking and laughing, they were surprised to find a silent, veiled woman barring their way into the conference room. Covering the door was a large banner on which was written, "We must risk unlearning what has kept us alive."

The veiled priestess bowed to them, indicating she would be their guide through the journey. "Welcome," she greeted them when all were waiting awkwardly before the covered door. "You must be women of great spirit and courage to have come here. We have been waiting for you. These are urgent times, and you are much needed. We are grateful you have come to create a future of power. Welcome. Few enter here, for this is a journey from which none return quite as they entered. Welcome, women of spirit and courage. If you wish to take this journey, please indicate your willingness by removing your shoes. None can walk this path in the shoes of the world from which you came."

The women quietly reached down and removed their shoes. When all had done so, the priestess sang a song from her Afro-Cuban tradition calling for Elegguèa, god of the crossroads, to open the way and make a safe passage for the initiates. Then she raised the banner covering the door and silently bade them enter.

Gate One: Entering Sacred Space, Evoking, and Exposition

Carrying their purses and other belongings, the women timidly entered the dark, candlelit room. The first thing they saw inside was the back of a figure cloaked in black, with arms outstretched barring the gate. Ye Ye Ife told the women they should knock at the gate by clapping their hands three times, as she beat the drum, to get the attention of the guardian.

I turned in response to their knocking. I was wearing a buzzard mask with a beak extending from my nose to my mouth and shiny black feathers rising up six inches above my hairline.[6] A voluminous black robe with gold trim covered all but my hands, which just stuck out from the large square cloth. I was no longer myself. I was carrying the archetypal energy of the guardian of the gates to the underworld.

"Who are you? Why do you come to my gate?" the guardian demanded.

The veiled priestess answered for the group, prompting them to join her. "We are women of spirit and imagination, here to create a future of power for women."

I surveyed the women assembled. "You?" I replied incredulously. "What folly! Do you know where you are? This is the path from which no one can return. Only the very foolish come here, or the very brave. This is the road to creating a future that is not based on the past, that is not consistent with the trends, that is not in any way reasonable—a future based in your collective imagination, born of your spirit." I looked at each woman closely. "Do you think such a future comes without a price?" I asked them.

"If you would enter here you must be willing to leave behind what you know of how the world is, for that is the old world of the patriarchy, which you are so good at negotiating. You must give up what you know works to create an unknown future of power and freedom for women.

"At these gates who you have known yourself to be, and how you know the world to be, will be stripped away. You will be left with nothing save your soul and your imagination. If you insist, you may take the journey. But no one can travel this path with all that baggage [indicating their purses, notebooks, etc.]. You must come here empty-handed.

"Enter at your own risk. You will have until the third bell to put down your belongings, indicating that you wish to remain. Or you may leave with no shame now. Once you pass through the next gate, the way back closes. After that you may not leave," I warned. "Choose."

With that I struck a Tibetan bell three times, slowly, allowing each tone to reverberate and die out while I waited for them to choose to enter or leave the initiation. To my surprise, all the women stayed.

Reflections

The preceding section was designed to allow women to choose powerfully whether or not they would surrender to the process, realizing that they must participate fully or not at all. If they had not chosen with full consciousness at the outset of the rite, the leaders would have encountered well-deserved resistance. This is a good example of the use of exposition early in a rite to orient participants to what will be expected of them, and what they may expect. By affirming their consent to continue, participants grounded themselves in the altered space.

At first some of the women treated it like a game they would not be required to give themselves over to playing for keeps. We heard them giggling uncomfortably in the hall outside the door as they assembled before being allowed to enter. Some were mildly annoyed at having to leave their shoes in the hallway, and put down their purses and notebooks. This did not discourage the leaders from the firmness of their stance. By staying firm and clear in our intentions, neither watering the rite down nor pandering to ambivalence, but giving participants freedom to stay or to leave, we created a rigorous environment that called the participants to meet us with full integrity.

For a rite to be feminist, women must be free to choose their participation. Yet rites of passage are matters of surrender built on trust. One can only be initiated by giving over control to the leader of the rite. This was a serious initiation rite, the only one covered in this book. It was not meant for the fainthearted. It was meant for women who, whatever their background, were earnest in their intent to create a future of power for women and willing to pay the price of doing so. Most of the participants were new to this sort of ritual, so we needed to make sure they were willing to face the challenge and probable discomfort. It would have been disruptive had an initiate changed her mind halfway through. For the participants to choose freely and commitedly, we had to make it clear that we were deadly serious, that it would not be comfortable, and that they would not return as they began.

The structure of this rite made the usual circle casting, invocations, and grounding superfluous. The space had been sanctified with burning herbs and prayer before the women entered what was already a strong container for ritual magic. In the null zone of the underworld there are no four directions, no elements, no points of orientation. Disorientation is the point. There was no need to invoke the Goddess; she was there in the persona of the guardian vulture.

This claim may seem blasphemous at worst, arrogant at best. The taking on of an archetypal energy or deity by a person does not occur in Bible-based religions. To those unfamiliar with the custom, it may seem evil or dangerous, like using the gods for one's own purposes. Or it may seem like playacting, innocent but foolish. In many shamanic practices, from the Afro-Brazilian practices of Yoruba and Santeria to tribal medicine work to Wicca, it is a common practice. What does it mean to carry divine persona or archetypal energy? What is the ontological foundation for such a claim?

Thought forms made of the primal creative energies of the universe, which cathect human consciousness and emotions, are called archetypes. The energy that makes up these thought forms is no different from the energy comprising any other form in the universe. It exists all around and through us. The thought forms, however, while created by human beings, take on a life of their own. The devil, for example, while merely a thought form created by people out of a dualistic paradigm, is a thought form that has been known to be evoked or invoked by satanic cults with terrifying results.

Likewise, the vulture who stands at the gates of transformation is a thought form that has existed in many symbol systems for thousands of years. Our bodies and memories respond to it because it is archetypal and nature based. It is a known thought form, archetype, and symbol, meaning that it is multidimensional and multivalent. To evoke such an archetype or thought form into oneself is to embody that particular energy. Anyone can do this. One has only to be willing to put aside one's ideas about who one is, and to open to a larger self that contains more than one's known identity.

The self is not solid. Only the shell of identity or personality pretends to be separate. The soul is at one with all that is. Therefore human beings are capable of opening to any energy, allowing it to move through them. How else would it be possible to feel another's pain or share their joy? Western psychology, built on an atomized notion of separate selves, does not allow for this phenomenon. So-called civilized people live their lives walled off from one another and from divine energies, except in extreme cases of what is usually understood as a psychotic break or a mystical experience. Yet the best actors know what mystics and shamans in all traditions have always known: it is possible to call in and open to energy and experience beyond one's personal scope.

This is what a tribal shaman does when calling in the spirits of the ancestors, and what I did in calling in the guardian of the underworld. Although anyone can do it, it is not an act to be taken casually or lightly, especially if one is dealing with such a powerful archetype of destruction/transformation as the vulture. Calling archetypal energies is a serious business. It should be reserved for experienced practitioners and done with the utmost integrity and rigor, or the energy can wreak havoc in one's life. ☉✇

Gate Two: Intention

We called on each woman to affirm her personal commitment by stating her name and her purpose. One by one the women came up to the gate to be challenged. I asked, "Who are you? Why do you come here?" Ye Ye Ife whispered her coaching into their ears. Each participant had to reply aloud with her own name and the phrase "to create a future of power and freedom for women" before being allowed to pass beneath the gauze archway. Once on the other side of the gate, the women waited in a small huddle for the others to arrive. When all had passed, their veiled guide took her drum and led them in a chant, "Down, down, decomposing, recomposing."[7] They wove around the room single file, chanting, until arriving at the gate again.

R e f l e c t i o n s ❦

By asserting her intentional presence and aligning her will with the magic we were there to perform, each woman placed herself at the center of the event. The reader may note that we were upping the ante. Following her choice to remain in the group came each woman's personal commitment to the group purpose. This sort of group alignment and personal responsibility for one's involvement may be the single most important factor in transformational or magical ritual. Without it there is no clear intention, and without clear intention there is no magic.[8] ☉✇

Gate Three: Purgation (Image)

Once more they knocked. The gatekeeper once again had her back to them. They must get her attention. They clapped three times. I turned.

"You again? And what do you want now?"

"We are women of spirit, here to create a future of power and freedom for women."

"Very well, but what will you sacrifice for such a wish? Do you think you can create such a future and still preserve your precious image? You must be willing to give up looking good. No woman was ever free who was stopped by her concern for how things look or what people will say. You will have to let go of keeping up appearances. Are you willing to do this? It is a big sacrifice. No more letting embarrassment stop you. You may have to look a fool from time to time.

"Now step forward."

The first woman stepped up to the gate. I asked her, "Are you willing to give up looking good?" When she assented, I asked her to remove all her jewelry. She handed it to Ye Ye Ife, who placed it in its own bag for safety and then into a basket. Once the initiate's jewelry was removed, I took a veil from a second basket and placed it over her head, indicating the removal of image, before sending her through the gate and receiving the next initiate.[9]

When all the women had passed, again they chanted, moving single file, "Down, down, decomposing, recomposing," around the room until reaching the fourth gate.

R e f l e c t i o n s

Gates one and two set up the structures of intention and commitment necessary to do the ritual work. Gate three began the process of purgation, stripping down all that was in the way of creation. When people try to create out of anything save emptiness, they re-create the past. That is why the rest of the gates each, in turn, strip something away that would be an impediment to our purpose: creating a future of power and freedom for women.

Gate Four: Purgation (Comfort)

Again the women knocked. Again I turned.

"So, you return to my gate. What do you want now?"

"We are women of spirit and imagination, here to create a future of freedom and power for women," they intoned.

"Ah, well then," I taunted them. "And do you think, should you find this future of power and freedom, that you would have any idea how to conduct yourselves in such a world? Let us suppose that you completed this rite and reentered the world to find it completely altered. Suppose what you found was a world of power and freedom for women. What then? Do you think you would be comfortable in such a world? I think not. You would have no idea what to do.

"People like things familiar. People do not like the new, the transformed. They do not mind the new, improved version as long as it is more and better of the same. But what you are asking for—that is unfamiliar. It makes people uncomfortable. You know how to get along in the world as it is. You would be very uncomfortable in such a different world.

"You cannot enter an unfamiliar future of freedom and remain in your world of comfort and familiarity. To enter such a world, you would have to step outside your comfort zone."

I regarded the first woman in the line. "Will you give up comfort and familiarity to enter a future you cannot yet see?" I asked. She nodded. Ye Ye Ife then took her by the shoulders, spun her around three times, and sent her through the gate backwards. I queried each woman in turn, and Ye Ye Ife sent each one spinning through the gate disoriented. They then began the chant again. "Down, down . . ."

Gate Five: Purgation (Despair and Resignation), and Creating Communitas

When the initiates reached the fifth gate and had again stated their purpose, they were told that this gate would require them to give up the familiar despair and cynicism that keep one from acting. In order to cross over they would be required to act together. No one could go through this gate alone; they must go through as a group. It was up to them to figure out how they would do it. They had until the third bell.

This is the point at which it became evident that these women were playing for keeps. There was no hemming and hawing, no jockeying for control, no taking care of anybody. Without speaking a word, before the second bell had rung, they formed themselves into a shape of entwined hands and arms. Acting as one, they moved through the gate with lightness and singleness of purpose. Something extraordinary had happened.

R e f l e c t i o n s

Often what prevents activists and visionaries from achieving success is despair and cynicism, or resignation. A world of evidence supports despair that no one will understand, cynicism about people not caring, or resignation that it has always been thus and it will never change. One is defeated before one begins if one is certain that she will get no cooperation, or that the noble cause will dissolve into petty squabbles and turf battles. Despair is the cry of the lone wolf.

Success in any venture requires alignment and cooperation. It is possible to give up despair and cynicism only inside a community of shared commitment. In evolution it is the cooperative who survive. Ritual provides an opportunity for the emergence of communitas, cynicism's antidote. Victor Turner tells us that "communitas breaks in through the interstices of structure in liminality; at the edges of structure, in marginality; and from beneath structure, in inferiority. It is almost everywhere held to be sacred or 'holy,' possibly because it transgresses or dissolves the norms that govern structured or institutionalized relationships and is accompanied by experiences of unprecedented potency."[10] At this gate, the initiates had to demonstrate their ability to cooperate in the spontaneous building of communitas. Only cooperation and alignment can face down despair and cynicism.

Gate Six: Purgation (Survival Strategies)

The women circled to the gate and knocked once more. They appeared stronger in their assertion of being women of spirit, there to create a future of freedom and power. As guardian of the gates, I surveyed them. They were ready, even eager. Their eyes were shining through their veils.

"Well," I began, "here is the moment you must give up something you think you cannot live without. There is something in your manner of negotiating the world that is so fundamental to who you are used to being that you may think it is who you are. It is not who you are. You are much, much more than that. But it may be what has kept you alive in the world you have known. In order to enter an unknown world you must leave behind your very method of survival. 'We must risk unlearning what has kept us alive. What are some of those things that have kept us alive?" I asked them.

A litany began. "Manipulation. Self-effacement. Being 'nice.' Being 'bitchy.' Hopelessness. Peacemaking. Deception. Silence." Women called out qualities, and all repeated what each had spoken. Spontaneously I decided to go for broke. I looked at my co-leader for assent. She seemed to sense what I sensed. The women were up to a larger challenge. We would not let them off the hook until each woman had identified and named for herself her own survival strategy. This was a major piece of work. It could take years in traditional psychotherapy, if it were broached at all. These initiates would accomplish it in ten minutes.

I named their task. Each woman would name and agree to unlearn the primary strategy that had kept her alive in patriarchal society before passing through the penultimate gate. I invited them to look at themselves and their lives, then step forward.

"What are you willing to risk unlearning that has kept you alive?" I queried.

"Silence," the first initiate replied. "I keep silent in the face of injustice. I am silent so that no one will notice me."

"Will you now speak even when it seems dangerous, even when you are sure it is a bad idea?" I challenged. "Because everything in you will tell you that it is, you know."

"Yes," she assented, nodding, "I will speak in the face of danger."

"You may pass," I told her, and let her walk between the gates.

The next woman said she would unlearn lying; another, withholding. They gave up complaining, being victims, being cute, coy, clever, reasonable, good, realistic, and cowardly. I no longer remember all that the women said. I do remember the quality of the honesty and courage that was present in their words and faces.

Once more they circled the room, chanting words that increased in meaning and power with each round of reinventing themselves. "Down, down, decomposing, recomposing."

R e f l e c t i o n s

Women, like all subordinated people, have developed strategies for survival. In a community of trust and shared purpose, it is possible to risk even those. This was the moment that the banner on the door portended. We were asking the women to risk unlearning what had kept them alive. This was the moment of transformation. This was the gate from which there is no road back.

Gate Seven: Purgation (Powerlessness)

Now came the turning point in the ritual. Having cleared away all that stood as an obstacle to their own power, the initiates could now give up the one thing that stood between them and their vision: their powerlessness. "It is so easy to be powerless," I chided. "So safe. There is no risk of making a mistake if you are powerless. If you take power, there is great risk. People could get angry. You could make a terrible mistake. You would have to be responsible for choices that affect the lives of others. Is it worth the risk? Consider: Only when you can stand powerfully in the face of the unknown and unrecognizable can you invent a new future," I asserted. "These are high stakes. It will take great courage to step into the power to invent the future."

I confronted them one by one.

"Will you give up shrouding your power and vision in order to create an unrecognizable future?"

One by one the women stepped forward. Yes and yes and yes. As each woman claimed her power I removed her veil. The initiates sprang through the final gate, uncovered faces open and alive. They could rejoin the world from a new place. They had survived the stripping away, and now they were ready to invent a future for women of power and spirit that was not based on the patriarchal past. A radical feminist nun said as her veil was removed, "I give up the veil for the second time."

Reflections

Perhaps what stands between women and their power is as thin as a veil, shrouding our magnificence in a film of image, comfort, resignation, and all the strategies we have designed for our own survival and simultaneous defeat. Yes, patriarchy exists, but we are its shadow. What would happen if women rose in communities to our full power and simply refused to collude with subjugation any longer, even by doing what we think has kept us alive? Not refusing with anger or blame, but simply by removing our veil and taking our power? What then? Something new might happen: a future of power and freedom, grounded in our common spirit.

Creation: Calling In the New

Ye Ye Ife greeted the initiates on the other side. She gently ushered each woman to the side of the room away from the gate, and had her lie down. When all were lying comfortably on the floor, she began to rhythmically beat the djembe. I began to lead the group in a visualization. I put them in a time machine and catapulted them to the year 2030. This was the future of freedom and power for women, I told them. If they could see nothing it was because we were inventing it now, from the future. It could be as they would have it. The only things certain were that in this future, women's bodies were worshiped as embodiments of the Goddess, and women's minds were fully respected. What did such a world look like? What else did they see there?[11]

I left them to invent in silence, while the drum beat steadily, until they were ready to return by opening their eyes and sitting up. When they did so they found the room filled with bright sunshine. I was no longer the darkly robed, masked guardian, but a woman like themselves, their friend and guide into a co-created future. Across the floor was a red line, the final limen of this liminal event. The women stood up and began to sway and move with the rhythm.

Declaration: Committing Ourselves

"Who will be first to share her vision and stand for an invented future?" The first woman came forward. "First I must blow the fairy dust on you," I told her, as I blew bubbles over her from a magic bubble wand. "Now enter your unrecognizable future."

She jumped across the line. "I stand for the end of violence against women," she declared.

"Yes," I responded. "And what would be present if there were an end to vio-lence against women?"

Her face broke out in a big smile. "A sense of security. I stand for a future in which women and children are safe to go anywhere."

"Go forth," I told her, as I marked her forehead with a woman symbol. "One's life is peculiarly one's own when one has invented it," I said, quoting feminist anar-chist foremother Emma Goldman, in the final litany to be repeated for each initi-ate. She danced over to the corner where Ye Ye Ife played the drum, where she was handed a rhythm instrument to play.

Raising Energy: Empowering Our Declaration

With each woman's declaration, the rhythm grew stronger. Women stood for a future of religious power for women, a world that supports the raising of chil-dren, a world with enough for everyone, a world of relatedness to all life, of health and wellness, a world in which women are the owners of their own bodies and souls. As each woman crossed the line and spoke, I marked her forehead. Finally all stood with instruments, dancing. Careful to stay on the side of the line that was the future, we began to dance more energetically. The beat grew stronger. We drummed and danced out visions into a cone of energy. Then we grounded it, dropping and placing our hands on the ground. "So be it. Make it so." I removed the limen on the floor. We were on the other side.

Dedication: Sending Forth

"The future is in your hands," I told them. "There will be much in the world that will give you evidence that what you have stood for today is impossible, or too dangerous to continue to stand for it. It is only your commitment and your sup-port of one another that will keep it in place, and continue to create it. Choose a buddy, a sister, who will hold you to what you spoke here today, and set up a time to reach one another."

The women stayed in the circle. They did not want to leave. I felt deeply moved by their courage and trust, and told them so. It had been a powerful experience, and I was aware of the great privilege they had afforded me in allowing me to lead them through such a journey. The women exchanged numbers, then slowly left the room. In an hour and fifteen minutes they had changed the future, if not for the world, at least for themselves.

* FEMINIST ANALYSIS *

In the weeks following the ritual, Ye Ye Ife spoke to several of the participants. They reported profound changes in various areas of their lives, from dreams to major spiritual awakenings. Some found the courage to follow paths they had previously feared. Others reported increased synchronicities. Some women spoke of taking more power and leadership in their religious communities. Women claimed to have a sharper eye for patriarchy, which they could now see without veils. One woman reported becoming more financially responsible. Freedom and possibility were present at a new level for many of the participants. One woman said, "It touched deep, nonverbal places in me. I am able to articulate thoughts out of my own experience now, rather than internalized beliefs from outside."

Transformational ritual reorganizes the very structures through which people think and act. It is no small undertaking. It requires a high level of responsibility and regard for the welfare, dignity, and choices of those who place their trust in such a process. It demands impeccability in which every detail is consistent. It demands high integrity of the leaders. All events conspire to lead up to one pivotal, liminal moment in which the initiate steps across a line of her own free will. The initiate is brought to the brink and asked to jump. The power to create the outcome then returns to the initiate.

Not all rituals are transformational. Many rituals bind participants to the moral order of our world as it is, and in that they serve a major social function. Such rituals are affirmational or confirmational. They affirm a connection or value that already exists. "They restore order when it has been lost."[12] The preponderance of rituals in the world of mainstream religion would fall into this category. They do not hope to transform anyone's relationship to the world, but to reaffirm it.

Feminists have no stake in reaffirming the existing patriarchal social order. They have a stake in transforming it. The purpose of this ritual was to transform participants in their fundamental mode of being, and thus to free their actions and imaginations for social transformation. Only after stripping away all that is in the way of choosing can an initiate choose, rather than having her old script choose, her future. Like a sculptor carving a piece of stone, transformational ritual removes all impediments to the beauty and power of the shape beneath. Only then can we create a world of power and freedom for women of spirit.

AIN'T I A WOMAN? A RITE OF PASSAGE

Some rituals come not at a time of year, but at a time of life. Nevertheless, they are temporal and reflect a change of season. All women have changes of season in their lives. These are inner changes of body and spirit as well as outward changes in role. In the ancient Greek and Celtic worlds these phases referenced the phases of the moon: maiden, mother, and crone. In those days women married young, often at or near the onset of fertility, and there was a clear demarcation between the stages of life. A maiden was simply an unmarried woman. For most women, the next phase of life involved being a mother. Many women died in childbirth, never living into old age, but those who passed menopause were wise women, or crones. They had a role in their culture of helping with the children, providing wise counsel.

In Barbara Myerhoff's comprehensive definition, "rites of passage are a category of rituals that mark the passages of an individual through the life cycle, from one stage to another over time, from one role or social position to another, integrating the human and cultural experiences with biological destiny: birth, reproduction, and death."[1] Rites of passage, marking social transitions into womanhood or manhood in primal cultures, aid the initiate in making the transition from one discrete stage of life to the next. This is the point at which the girl or boy is introduced to her or his culture's idea of being a woman or a man, and is instructed on the commensurate rights and responsibilities.

Such rites, according to Myerhoff, provide teaching moments, "when the society seeks to make the individual most fully its own, weaving group values and understandings into the private psyche so that internally provided individual motivation replaces external controls."[2] For better or for worse, young people were taught the rules of sex and gender according to the common wisdom of their society in this way until quite recently. These practices continue in many tribal cultures today.

Such rites of passage are a two-edged sword. On the one hand, they facilitate an all-important transition, providing youth with needed instruction and recognition by their elders, and eventually incorporating them into the common life and mores of the tribe. With no such rites practiced in our culture, North American young people are generally at the mercy of the media and their peers to tell them how to be a woman or a man. This may be a significant factor in the breakdown of common culture.

On the other hand, many of these rites and rules have been and are oppressive to women in the extreme. They revolve around preparing young girls for and indoctriniating them into their subordinate role as sexual and domestic slaves. The boys are often indoctrinated into a culture of domination. Frequently they are torn away from the women, especially their mothers and female peers, and "reborn" into an all-male warrior society, which can even include using prepubescent girls as mistresses before the genital mutilation that "prepares" the girls for marriage and motherhood.[3]

While mild remnants of social puberty rites exist in the Jewish bar mitzvah (or the afterthought concession to feminism, the bas mitzvah), the Christian confirmation, the wedding ceremony, and associated rituals, passages through life's stages are not formally recognized, by and large, in today's modern world. Most especially, transitions from childhood into the sexuality of womanhood or manhood often go unmarked by any official initiation or instruction in what is expected of an adult member of society and a sexual person. Consequently, young people are likely to devise their own informal, ad hoc rites of passage. These consist of a variety of unsupervised, dangerous activities such as taking drugs, engaging in daredevil stunts in cars, performing various unsafe sexual acts, and sometimes perpetrating physical violence toward young people of other ethnic or sexual groups. The absence of rites in secular culture is a void in young people's psyches that they grope to fill, often at great personal and societal cost.

Clearly something is needed to help both women and men take the leap from biological to social womanhood or manhood. The question is how to devise rites that allow for gender freedom, while providing the ground for common value and moral instruction in citizenship; when and by whom such rites should be performed; and whether it is even possible to create an initiation rite sufficiently powerful to "work," without risking the safety of the young person involved.

The question is made more confusing by the wide disparity between biological and social transitions in postindustrial society. In primal cultures, while social womanhood may not correspond exactly to the onset of menses, there is at some point an irreversible rite of passage into social womanhood. In any given culture the time and meaning of that rite is agreed upon. Often social puberty rites constitute an entrance into the world of sexual activity, which comes packaged with instruction and taboos.[4]

In today's Western culture, there is no initiation or instruction into the world of sexual mysteries, no set of responsibilities or taboos passed down, no acknowledgment, even, of this momentous step. In her book on coming of age in the wake of the sexual revolution, Naomi Wolf powerfully articulates the need for older women to initiate younger women into womanhood through a series of challenges. Womanhood's rights and rites ought to be earned through tests of strength and accomplishment, or else, as Wolf points out, womanhood ends up being defined, not by women, but by boys, who set the measures for a girl's incipient womanhood based on their responses.[5]

What constitutes social womanhood in postmodern America? First sexual intercourse? First driver's license? High school graduation? College graduation? Pregnancy? Marriage? Financial or domestic independence? None of these provides an adequate answer to the questions what is a woman, and how and by whom does the mysterious state of womanhood get conferred? Menses arrives earlier and earlier, but most women are marrying later, if they marry at all. They may or may not stay married. Married or not, they may or may not choose motherhood. Many women are living well past menopause into old age, outliving husbands by many years, with no passage and no social role awaiting or honoring them. Are they not still women?

Postindustrial Western society has no clear point for ritualizing the onset of womanhood. Given the multilayered nature of women's social roles in our society, the categories of maiden, mother, and crone, despite their charm, may not apply to many women's lives anymore. I, for example, am not a mother. Neither did I marry until past the usual childbearing age. Was I a maiden, then, until I was forty? Am I now a mother, though childless? Is my friend who had a hysterectomy at thirty-five a crone? What about a divorced, childless woman? Does she revert to maiden? It is no wonder women are confused.

Yes, there are seasons in a woman's life. The onset of menses does signal a change, but we hope it is not yet a change from maiden to mother. And as a busy, healthy professional woman, I am not ready to be called a crone or even to play the role of wise woman, although I am nearing the age of menopause. I am stepping into a new season, but what to call it? How may women mark the seasons in their lives, so that they can move ahead when it is time? These questions are poignantly raised in the letter below, which inspired this ritual of womanhood.

* RITUAL DESCRIPTION *

My friend Wanda Lee felt a need for a rite of passage in her life and community when she was thirty-three. This need was apparently independent of any biological or social event. She had not become engaged or married. She was not pregnant. She was a businesswoman living in San Francisco with many friends. But, as she said so eloquently in the letter below, she had a sense that something was missing in her sense of herself as a woman, something that would have been provided in a more traditional culture. She asked me to help her with a rite of passage into womanhood that could include all women. Her purpose was for those present to feel acknowledged as women in their own right, regardless of their age, race, or marital status. It was a passage for women into the adult state of being a woman.

This is the letter she sent to invite people to the rite:

Dear Friends,

I am writing this letter to you as a special invitation. As a single professional female who has come very far from the youngest daughter in a family of nine in Detroit, Michigan, with still many places to go, I have been missing a certain something in my life and it's not necessarily to do with any thing or body, as it is more to do with self.

Most of my adult life has been in pursuit of womanhood. It didn't happen when I got my period, or wore a bra and later experienced cleavage. It didn't happen when I graduated from high school or college, or even the first time I fell in love and had sex. So I thought for sure it would happen when I got my first apartment or car, or the first time I cooked a home-cooked meal and had friends over for dinner on my "make-your-Momma-proud" table setting. No matter what accomplishment or threshold I crossed, whenever I looked into the mirror the reflection I saw was that of an uncertain girl.

So here I am at the age of thirty-three, and for the longest time I thought I had to wait until I was married or had children in order for womanhood to be secured. As a friend once told me, "I want you to have an experience that is beyond verbal description," i.e. marriage, children. Since I have been exploring this conversation, I have met and talked to several women who have and have not crossed these thresholds, older and younger, and still do not feel it for themselves. I have learned that marriage gives you wifery and childbirth gives you motherhood; womanhood in its purest essence may or may not accompany.

You might say that we're in search of our mothers' gardens. That self-generative, nurturing, spiritual, loving, strengthening, beautiful, co-creating, powerful place we call "Womanhood!" That place where through intuition we know what to do, where to do, how to do, and how much to do—naturally. That place that is beyond verbal description.

I recently have found that place and would like to share this experience with my female friends who have had the same conversation. I am creating this event around acknowledgment—a rite-of-passage, if you will. This day is not just for women, it's for girls, and teenagers, and young women, and mothers, and daughters, and sisters, and aunts, and girlfriends, and grandmothers and great-grandmothers and great-great-grandmothers, and Misses and Mrs. It's for every woman and woman to be.

In the tradition of my female African ancestors and the hunting and gathering societies of all cultures before us, the women have always gathered together to share,
acknowledge, and celebrate one another. I hope you will share this day with me.

What would such a rite look like? We were inventing a rite of passage for adult
women who were, both biologically and socially, already women. The participants
would represent many different subcultures and socioeconomic groups. They
would range in age and marital status from unmarried professional women in
their twenties and thirties to a widowed grandmother in her seventies. They
would be African American, Asian, and Caucasian. They would represent evangelical and mainline Christian, New Age, Neopagan, and secular humanist religious
traditions. These were not likely to be women who would easily join hands and
sing in a circle. They might actually be uncomfortable in such a setting. Most of
them, Wanda informed me, would never have attended a women's ritual before.
We would need to invent a form that fit the content and the group.

What seemed appropriate under the circumstances was a ritual recognition of
what had already occurred and existed, but might have passed unnoticed: our
womanhood. What Wanda wanted was "for each and every woman to leave with a
sense of acknowledgment for her growth and the contribution she already was" to
her community. The central message of the ritual was: There is nowhere to "get" in
order to be "real women." We are already there. We are women—together and
separately, in all our forms and manners. By definition, then, everything we do is
womanly.

This idea of claiming our own womanhood broke through a stereotype that
keeps women enslaved to patriarchy, which is continually promoting new and better ways to "achieve" womanhood or femininity. The transition we were making
was not from girl to woman or from maiden to mother; rather, it was from trying
and striving to be a woman according to some externally imposed (male) definition, to recognizing ourselves as women, just as we are. The ritual opened up the
possibility that women might have the freedom to simply be.

Creating Sacred Space

The space we would be using was a large common area, recreational space in a
condominium. It consisted of three adjoining furnished areas separated by arch-
ways. The space, being such a distinct container in itself, suggested itself as a
sacred space to be used as it was. Of course, we moved furniture. Such a space did
not lend itself to a circle. Rather, it called for three distinct stages of the ritual.

Rites of passage generally involve separation from the society of the initiate's former life, a transitional phase, and a reincorporation phase, in which the initiate is reintegrated into her new role and society. We designed our rite in accordance with the space we were using, using van Gannep's three phases corresponding to the three distinct areas we were using.

The first area was preliminal, that is, the area before the liminal, or threshold, space. In this room we would have the "rites of separation from a previous world."[6] This was the room for meeting and greeting. The guests would be welcomed with water and fruit to refresh them, as a sort of preliminal cleansing. There they could chat among themselves, fill out and exchange recipes for everything from apple pie to stress reduction, and give their potluck food for the dinner to one of the designated servers, who would take it through the kitchen and, at the appropriate time, to the buffet table. By taking the food from the guests when they arrived, instead of having them place it on the buffet, we allowed them to remain in the preliminal space until we moved as a group into the next room. We arranged this first anteroom with comfortable chairs, a bowl of fruit, and a pitcher of water. Barbie dolls were scattered around the area, indicating the images of femininity from which the women were separating themselves. Between areas one and two, the archway was covered with butcher paper, making it impossible to walk through. This emphasized the limen, or threshold, through which we were breaking, in breaking with the stereotypes of women's pasts. It could also represent breaking the hymen to social womanhood.

The second area was the liminal space in which the women would create the central symbol of transition and self-recognition. We removed the chairs, leaving a large empty space and a large table where we laid a quilt base in preparation for creating our central symbol. I arranged an altar of goddess figures and other empowerment objects from a variety of cultures. On it I included a carved Afro-Cuban figure, a handsewn Pacha Mama from South America, a Chinese Quan Yin, a Middle Eastern Asherah, and an old European goddess of Willendorf. On the wall above the altar hung two poems which Wanda had copied and blown up to poster size, one by Nikki Giovanni, the other by Maya Angelou. This area was set to contain the threshold rites, the central rites, and symbol of claiming and affirming ourselves as women.

The final room was set for a communal feast in celebration of all the women who had contributed to the lives of the participants. We set tables with a place for each woman present. At each place was sheet music for the final song of the ritual, which the women would sing together. The food was arranged on another table buffet style. In one corner of that room, near the dining table, we set an altar with photographs of women we wished to honor.

Gathering and First Words: Welcome, Exposition, and Purgation

When most of the women were assembled comfortably in the anteroom, Wanda began. She stood on a chair in front of the white butcher paper and shouted "Welcome!" to get her guests' attention. Then she began to share the story of her search for womanhood, always thinking a woman was something that she was not, something she must attain.

She started to list all the things she had been told a woman was: demure, wise, sexy, full-breasted, manipulative, motherly. Then she invited her guests to list what they had thought a woman was supposed to be. All these she wrote in brightly colored marker on the butcher paper. When the group had listed all the characteristics they could think of, Wanda shared what she had discovered: A woman is what she says she is, no more, no less. Womanhood is what each of us dares to claim for ourselves.

All those images we carry were made up by somebody else. They are not "the truth." The truth was in this room, all the living, breathing women with children and parents and lovers and jobs and lives. "We are women, That's what I saw. I don't have to do anything to be a woman, I am one!" she laughed. By that point the butcher paper was covered with words of what women are "supposed" to be. "Who would like to join me in breaking through all this hogwash?" Wanda asked her friends. They laughed and jumped and ripped through the butcher paper, shouting, "I am a woman!"

Reflections

Mary Collins, Mary Daly, and Lesley Northup all speak of the power to name. What could be more fundamental than the right and power of to name ourselves as women? In defiance of every male-defined institution from psychology to advertising, these women dared to take back their right to define their own womanhood. In so doing they reclaimed the fundamental power of selfhood. This is the ground on which all other power rests: the power to say who one is for oneself. Without this power women may achieve economic and political equality yet never the genuine ontological freedom and autonomy that derive from the power to define.[7]

Invoking Presence

I awaited the women on the other side of the butcher paper. As they entered the sunny, empty room I smudged them with sage and invited them to slowly and silently mill around the room, noticing the other women there. As they milled I led a walking meditation based on a Buddhist practice called the four abodes of the Buddha, adapted by Joanna Rogers Macy as "Learning to See Each Other." The four abodes developed by the practice are "lovingkindness, compassion, joy in the joy of others, and equanimity."

First the women simply walked around, taking note of the other women with whom they were sharing the day, acknowledging discomfort in an urge to laugh or look away. I invited them to gaze at one another as they passed, considering that the opportunity to behold the uniqueness of this person they might never see again was given to them in this moment. Then I asked them to stop in front of the woman closest to them and to look into her eyes without speaking or touching.

"In this moment the privilege of beholding this woman is given to you. As you look at her, allow yourself to open to the gifts and strengths that lie behind those eyes—unmeasured reserves of ingenuity and endurance, of wit and wisdom. There are gifts there of which this woman herself may be unaware. Consider how much she has to give to our world. As you consider that, allow yourself to become aware of how much you desire that this woman be free from fear . . . and free from hatred and greed. Allow yourself to realize how you wish for her freedom from sorrow and the causes of suffering. And know that what you are now experiencing is the great lovingkindness. It is good for building a world."

I then invited them to nonverbally acknowledge their partner and to move on, stopping in front of someone else. I did this four times in all, once for each of the four abodes mentioned above. In the second abode, compassion, I invited them to become present to the disappointments, griefs, and losses behind one another's eyes—the pain that is there in each of us beyond the telling. In the third, they opened to the possibility for shared joy in creation, seeing what the other might offer. Finally, in the fourth abode, they allowed their consciousness to open to the "deep web of relationship that underlies and underweaves all experiencing, . . . the web of life in which you have taken being and in which you are supported . . . from which you cannot fall." I suggested that they allow themselves to feel gratitude to the women past and present who shared and sustained this great web, and to feel the assurance and the trust of placing our world in one another's hands. I asked them to consider that the person upon whom they gazed could be instrumental in the creation of new possibilities for all women.[8]

Reflections

This meditation, while in no way calling on deity or the four elements as we usually conceive them, called forth the divine in our ability to see the sacred in one another. I would say if we consider the Goddess to be immanent, we did indeed call on her. Certainly we invoked the sacred.

Creating a Central Symbol

After joining together in a call-and-response chant, we moved to the creation of the central symbol. There was a quilt frame on a large table. Wanda had asked each woman to bring a swatch of fabric having sentimental value, to be sewn into a common quilt and given to the Oakland Museum. She began with her swatch of denim from short cutoffs, telling how she had worn them and what had happened in them. I had a piece of antique silk velvet from a dress in which I had danced until dawn. Other women shared their stories of incipient and mature womanhood, pinning them onto the frame where they would be woven together to make a patchwork quilt that told of the variety of women's experiences and ways of being, all legitimate, all valid.

Reflections

The quilt was a celebration of women's diversity and particularity. Lesley Northup points out that "as women's crafts have taken on metaphorical power in women's ritualizing, so too have the homely objects and abilities that reflect female domestic expertise. Rituals of sewing, quilting, banner making, and so on take place in a spiritual context in many women's groups." Northup also observes that women's ritualizing seeks to include multiple perspectives.[9] It is noteworthy, then, that a homey symbol common to all American women, the quilt, allowed for an expression of inclusivity in this diverse group.

Creation: Calling In the New and Raising Energy

After we had completed our contributions to the quilt, Wanda again took the floor, and speaking from her heart to and about the women there assembled, acknowledged each of them for who they are and what they provide for her in her life. As a way of sealing the acknowledgment, one of the guests then read the Nikki Giovanni and the Maya Angelou poems on the wall, ending with Angelou's "I'm a woman/Phenomenally,/Phenomenal woman, That's me."[10]

This was a way of invoking a new, self-affirming sense of ourselves as women, replacing the old sense of not being enough, which the women had left behind in the first room. All the women took rhythm instruments from the corner and began to play and dance, raising energy for their newfound self-affirmation. Then they processed, one by one, into the third, postliminal, space.

Affirmation: Acknowledging, Communing, and Completing

At the threshold of the third room, each woman was blessed with a scented oil applied to her palm. She was then invited to help herself to food and nonalcoholic drinks and be seated. One of the women said a blessing over the food, and we ate. Then began a round of toasts to women present and absent, living and dead, in which each woman had the opportunity to raise her glass to the women in her life who had inspired and supported her. It is worth mentioning that many women acknowledged their mothers and other older female family members, again corroborating Northup's observation that women's rituals often have a place for naming and the honoring of elders.[11]

We completed the round of toasts by singing a tribute to the long line of women who have shared and influenced our lives. This completed the formal part of the ritual.

✳ FEMINIST ANALYSIS ✳

What did this ritual accomplish for the women who participated in it? Did they, through their participation, find validation, acknowledgment, and the freedom to be themselves? If so, how did that validation and freedom show itself in their lives? Did they go forward with more confidence in their work? Were their relationships, especially those with other women, empowered? Did they value themselves and their own experience at a deeper level? If so, how did that manifest itself?

As is so often the case with women's rites, we don't know for certain. In a primal rite of transition, the evidence for effective change lies not merely in the subjective feelings and experience of the initiates, but in their actual observable behavior prior to and following the rite, whose change is supported by the social structure at large. To ascertain ritual efficacy as evidenced by more than "feeling empowered," we would need ways of documenting transformation and empowerment with clear links to the ritual event. Perhaps we would even need double-blind studies, like those used in medicine, to demonstrate a direct relationship between outcomes and ritual events, independent of other intervening variables.

While we cannot say for certain that the rite directly caused any of the outcomes attributed to it by participants, there is anecdotal evidence that it may indeed have empowered some of the women in significant ways. In the past fifteen months, since the ritual took place, the following events occurred in the lives of the participants:

Two of the women who attended were inspired to hold similar events to which they invited community members to bring and share pieces of their lives.

Three of the women who were single at the time of the ritual have entered into committed relationships with men. While this is not necessarily a sign of empowerment, Wanda (who at the time of this writing plans to marry the man she became involved with shortly after the women's rite) asserts that the rite allowed her to acknowledge herself as a whole woman. Finally believing she was "woman enough to be lovable," by just being herself, made room in her psyche for a significant other who loves her for herself, she believes. Some of the women who attended say that their relationships among themselves have deepened, as well. Wanda also tells me that as a result of getting a truer sense of her worth, she left a dead-end job and took a better job, doubling her income in the following year.

I am most moved by the story of a woman who placed a photograph of her deceased sister on the altar when we were toasting women not present. She had been out of touch with her sister's family since her sister's death some years earlier. Following the ritual, she got in touch with her teenage nieces and is now helping to raise and empower them to grow into strong women with a sense of self-worth.

Mary Collins states, "Women's personhood, spiritual and social identity, authority, creativity, destiny—not immediate economic or political power—are the controlling concerns of effective feminist liturgy."[12] This feminist ritual, by addressing those very concerns, allowed the personhood and social identities of a diverse group of women *as women* to emerge and attain recognition. As the women looked into each other's eyes, they affirmed the sanctity and validity of each woman's unique and complete womanhood in all the seasons of her life.

NOTES

Preface

1. Simone de Beauvoir, *The Second Sex* (New York: Alfred A. Knopf, 1953) xvi, sums up the long-standing cultural assumption: Woman "is defined and differentiated with reference to man and not he with reference to her; she is the incidental, the inessential, as opposed to the essential. He is the Subject, he is the Absolute—she is the Other."
2. See Ronald L. Grimes, "Infelicitous Performances and Ritual Criticism," in *Ritual Criticism* (Columbia: University of South Carolina Press, 1990).
3. This term will be developed in another project, *The Future of God,* whose publication is pending.

1. She Who Rules the Symbols Rocks the World

1. Z. Budapest, *Holy Book of Women's Mysteries* (Berkeley, Calif.: Wingbow Press, 1974), *Grandmother of Time* (San Francisco: HarperSanFrancisco, 1989), and *Summoning the Fates* (New York: Harmony, 1998); Mary Daly, *Beyond God the Father* (Boston: Beacon Press, 1973); Monica Sjöö and Barbara Mor, *The Great Cosmic Mother: Rediscovering the Religion of the Earth* (San Francisco: HarperSanFrancisco, 1991); Merlin Stone, *When God Was a Woman* (New York: Dorset Press, 1976); Carol Christ, "Why Woman Need the Goddess," *Womanspirit Rising,* ed. Carol Christ and Judith Plaskow (New York: Harper & Row, 1979), originally given as keynote address at "The Great Goddess Re-Emerging" conference, University of California at Santa Cruz, 1978; Starhawk, *The Spiral Dance* (New York: Harper & Row, 1979).
2. For a study of what these groups are doing and what they have in common, see Lesley Northup, *Ritualizing Women: Patterns of Spirituality* (Cleveland: The Pilgrim Press, 1997).
3. Estimates vary widely, from 250,000 to as many as nine million women tortured and sacrificed during the Burning Times (a term referring to the witch burnings of the Inquisition; in common usage in Neopagan and Wiccan circles, it probably has its origins in Gardnerian Witchcraft lore of the 1950s in Britain). No one really knows. There are records showing that the first trials for witchcraft took place in 1022 in Orlèans, France. The papal bull making witchcraft a heresy punishable by death was issued in 1484, the same year that Dominicans Kramer and Springer published the illustrious Malleus Maleficarum text for the identification and destruction of witches and heretics. The first woman officially burned for the crime of worshiping a deity other than the Christian God was Dame Alice Kyteler, executed in 1324, according to Margaret Murray, *God of the Witches* (Oxford University Press, 1931; reprinted 1960 by Doubleday, Garden City, N.Y.), 21–22. The burnings continued well into the eigh-

teenth century, and the laws remained in effect until 1957, when the laws in England were finally repealed.

4. Susan Maloney, Ph.D., spoken during a class on feminist theological ethics, Immaculate Heart College Center, 1995.

5. For my definition of feminism I refer to Gerda Lerner, *Creation of Patriarchy* (New York: Oxford University Press, 1986). Lerner points out that the term covers a broad spectrum, including: "(a) a doctrine advocating social and political rights for women equal to those of men; (b) an organized movement for the attainment of these rights; (c) the assertion of the claims of women as a group and the body of theory women have created; (d) belief in the necessity of large-scale social change in order to increase the power of women" (p. 236).

6. Mary Collins, "Principles of Feminist Liturgy," in *Women at Worship,* ed. Marjorie Procter-Smith and Janet Walton (Louisville, Ky.: Westminster/John Knox Press, 1993), 15.

7. See Helene P. Foley, ed., *The Homeric Hymn to Demeter* (Princeton, N.J.: Princeton University Press, 1994), for the most up-to-date translation, with feminist commentary, of the ancient Greek myth.

8. For a reconstruction of the Semitic goddess hidden between the lines, see Raphael Patai, *The Hebrew Goddess,* 3d ed. (Detroit: Wayne State University Press, 1990).

9. The term "subjugated voice" was coined by Michel Foucault, *The History of Sexuality* (New York: Vintage Books, 1990). Regarding Mary, see, for example, Kenneth L. Woodward, "Hail, Mary," *Newsweek,* 25 August 1997, 48–55. He notes that "the twentieth century has belonged to Mary. From almost every continent, visionaries have reported more than 400 'apparitions' of the Virgin—more than in the previous three centuries combined." Queenship Press, Santa Barbara, California, publishes many of the books on this subject.

10. Collins, "Principles of Feminist Liturgy," 11.

11. Monique Wittig, *Les Guerillères,* trans. David Le Vay (New York: Avon Books, 1973), 89.

12. Marija Gimbutas, *The Language of the Goddess* (San Francisco: Harper & Row, 1989).

2. Reality in the Shape of a Woman

1. Barbara Myerhoff, "Rites of Passage: Process and Paradox," in *Celebration,* ed. Victor Turner (Washington, D.C.: Smithsonian Institution Press, 1982), 109.

2. Victor Turner, "Brain, Body, and Culture," in *The Anthropology of Performance* (New York: PAJ Publications, 1986), 156–78.

3. Myerhoff, "Rites of Passage," 121; John E. Pfeiffer, *The Creative Explosion* (Ithaca, N.Y.: Cornell University Press, 1985).

4. Marija Gimbutas, *The Language of the Goddess* (San Francisco: Harper & Row, 1989). See also Pfeiffer, *Creative Explosion.*

5. Tom F. Driver, "Ritualizing: The Animals Do It and So Do We," in *The Magic of Ritual* (San Francisco: HarperSanFrancisco, 1991), 31.

6. Gregory Bateson and Mary Catherine Bateson, *Angels Fear* (New York: Bantam Books, 1988), 152–56.

7. Mary Daly, *Beyond God the Father* (Boston: Beacon Press, 1973), 13.

8. Collins, "Principles of Feminist Liturgy," 20.

9. See Patricia Monaghan, *O Mother Sun!* (San Francisco: HarperSanFrancisco, 1994), for stories of solar goddesses.

10. Oothoon, "Evocation of the Goddess," *Green Egg* 9, no. 69 (March 21, 1975).

11. It is this belief about women's excessive sexuality that is used to justify female "circumcision," in the cultures that practice it, as a means of keeping women faithful to their husbands.

12. For further discussion, see John A. Phillips, *Eve: The History of an Idea* (New York: Harper & Row, 1984), 160–69.

13. Catherine Keller, *From a Broken Web* (Boston: Beacon Press, 1986), 205–6.

14. Sarah Pomeroy, *Goddesses, Whores, Wives, and Slaves: Women in Classical Antiquity* (New York: Schocken Books, 1975).

15. Wendy Hunter Roberts and Rick Hamouris, "Invocation of the Goddess," Written for the Saturday-night Walpurgisnacht part of the Beltane (1991). This ritual is described in chapter 7.

16. Roberts and Hamouris, "Invocation of the Wounded God," ibid.

17. These two paragraphs are adapted from Wendy Hunter Roberts, "In Her Name," in *Women at Worship: Interpretations of North American Diversity,* ed. Marjorie Procter-Smith and Janet R. Walton (Louisville: Westminster/John Knox, 1993).

3. Cauldron of Rebirth: Halloween

1. To the best of my knowledge, as no basis for the holiday can be found in Hebrew or Greek scripture, there is no Protestant equivalent. The Jewish tradition fulfills some of the same ritual functions nearer to the autumnal equinox, at Rosh Hashanah.

2. Mircea Eliade, *A History of Religious Ideas from the Stone Age to the Eleusinian Mysteries* (Chicago: University of Chicago Press, 1978).

3. James Melaart, *Çatal Hüyük: A Neolithic Town in Anatolia* (London: Thames & Hudson, 1967). Elinor Gadon, *The Once and Future Goddess: A Symbol for Our Time* (San Francisco: Harper & Row, 1989), ch. 6. Anodea Judith, "Peruvian Pilgrimage," *Green Egg* 24, no. 93: 20–21.

4. Ernest Klein, *A Comprehensive Etymological Dictionary of the English Language,* vol. 2, L–Z (Amsterdam: Elsevier Publishing Company, 1967). Otter Zell, editor of *The Green Egg,* said in a 1992 telephone conversation that Margot Adler had given him this information. For the 1985 figure, see Margot Adler, *Drawing Down the Moon,* rev. ed. (Boston: Beacon Press, 1986), 455.

5. Anodea Judith, "The Crone Song," *Welcome to Annwfn,* audiocassette (Redwood Valley, Calif.: Nemeton Publishing, 1986).

6. Beth Boneblossom of the Reclaiming Collective, San Francisco, "Cauldron of Changes," chant heard in ritual.

7. Chant heard in ritual, author unknown.

8. "All from Air into Air," by Gwydian Pendderwen, Church of All Worlds Inc.

9. For several of the classic discussions of these issues, see Sherry Ortner, "Is Female to Male as Nature Is to Culture?" in *Women and Values,* ed. Marilyn Pearsall (Belmont, Calif.: Wadsworth, 1986). See also essays in special issue of *Hypatia,* "Ecological Feminism," ed. Karen J. Warren (spring 1991), passim. See also Susan Griffin in *Woman and Nature: The Roaring inside Her* (New York: Harper & Row, 1978). See also *Reweaving the World: The Emergence of Ecofeminism,* ed. Irene Diamond and Gloria Orenstein (San Francisco: Sierra Club Books, 1990).

10. See Gadon, *The Once and Future Goddess,* chap. 13, "The Goddess Within: A Source of Empowerment for Women."

11. See Susan Faludi, *Backlash: The Undeclared War against American Women* (New York: Crown Publishers, 1991), 300–311, for her critique of men's movement spokesmen Warren Farrell and Robert Bly.

12. Robert Bellah, speaking at the American Academy of Religion national meeting, San Francisco, November 1997.

13. Carol Christ, *Diving Deep and Surfacing: Women Writers on Spiritual Quest* (Boston: Beacon Press, 1980). See also Starhawk, *Dreaming the Dark: Magic, Sex, and Politics* (Boston: Beacon Press, 1982); Gadon, *The Once and Future Goddess.*

4. Out of the Darkness: The Winter Solstice

1. Elinor Gadon, *The Once and Future Goddess* (San Francisco: HarperSanFrancisco, 1989), 346.

2. Rick Hamouris, "We Are a Circle," in *Welcome to Annwfn,* side 1.

3. Anodea Judith, "To the Crone," unpublished invocation.

4. Verses 1–3 of Frankie Armstrong, "Out of the Darkness," a song I learned as part of a ritual. I have taken the liberty of transposing the second and third verses, as more befitting this ritual.

5. Northup, *Ritualizing Women,* 23.

6. Jose Pintauro, "Blessing of the Water," in *The Earth Mass* (New York: Harper & Row, 1973).

7. Northup, *Ritualizing Women,* chap. 2.

8. Jose Pintauro, "Blessing of the Bread," in *The Earth Mass.*

9. Ramon Sender, "Oh Sun," in *Being of the Sun* (New York: Harper & Row, 1973). Adapted from the ancient Egyptian "Hymn to the Sun" by Akhenaton.

10. This is a chant by an unknown author, which I heard in a Church of All Worlds ritual.

11. Marija Gimbutas, *The Goddesses and Gods of Old Europe, 6500 to 3500 B.C.E.* (Berkeley: University of California Press, 1982).

12. Judith Ochshorn, *The Female Experience and the Nature of the Divine* (Bloomington: Indiana University Press, 1981).

13. Aeschylus, *Eumenides,* in The Complete Greek Drama, vol. 1, ed. Whitney Oakes and Eugene O'Neill Jr., trans. E. D. A. Morshead (New York: Random House, 1938), 297.

14. Sallie McFague, *The Body of God* (Minneapolis: Fortress Press, 1993).

15. Aristotle, *Genesis of Animals,* 4:4, 735A14–16.

16. Springer and Kramer, *Malleus Maleficarum* (Brussels: Culture et Civilisation, republished 1969), part one, question 6.

5. A Little Bit of Light: Candlemas

1. Pauline Campanelli, *Wheel of the Year* (St. Paul, Minn.: Llewelyn, 1989)

2. Mary Grigolia, "I Know This Rose," in *Commitment to a Vision* (Berkeley: self-published, 1989).

3. Northup, *Ritualizing Women,* 32. Northup, Caron, and Sered all emphasize the primacy of the ordinary in women's ritualizing.

4. Joanna Rogers Macy, *Despair and Personal Power in the Nuclear Age* (Philadelphia: New Society Publishers, 1983), 4–6.

5. For movement from past to future, see chapter 9, "Seven-Gated Passage: Autumn Equinox." For movement from despair to empowerment, see Macy, *Despair and Personal Power.* For movement from what is to what will be, see chapter 6, "Cakes for the Queen of Heaven." For movement from emptying out to taking in, see chapter 3, "Cauldron of Rebirth: Halloween."

6. Hamouris and Roberts, "A Little Bit of Light," unpublished song, 1992.

7. Collins, "Principles of Feminist Liturgy," 11.

8. Ibid. According to Northup, *Ritualizing Women,* women's ritualizing "fosters spontaneity, making allowance for the unanticipated" (p. 45).

9. Grimes, *Ritual Criticism,* chap. 1.

10. Northup, *Ritualizing Women,* points out that another feature common to women's ritualizing across cultures is "an emphasis on the body as a vital, inexhaustible, and beautiful symbolic source" (p. 31).

11. Collins, "Principles of Feminist Liturgy," 14–15.

6. Cakes for the Queen of Heaven: The Spring Equinox

1. For extensive research and analysis on all aspects of the Demeter/Persephone saga, see Helene P. Foley, "Gender Conflict and the Cosmological Tradition," in *The Homeric Hymn to Demeter* (Princeton, N.J.: Princeton University Press, 1994), 112–17.

2. Nancy Chodorow, "Family Structure and Feminine Personality," in *The Homeric Hymn to Demeter,* ibid.

3. Foley, "Gender Conflict and the Cosmological Tradition," 112–17.

4. Paula Wallowitz, "She's Been Waiting."

5. Anna Dembska, "A Circle Is Cast" (Cambridge, Mass.: Libana Inc., 1986).

6. I never use song books or song sheets if I can help it, because I believe it takes the worshiper's focus away from the group and into the printed matter. I have noticed that

singing is bolder and more expressive when people have nothing in their hands or blocking their faces.

7. This is a feature of feminist ritual to which both Mary Collins, in "Principles of Feminist Liturgy," and Lesley Northup, *Ritualizing Women,* refer.

8. "Return Again," words by Rafael Simka Kahn, music by Schlomo Carlebach, chant learned in Church of All Worlds ritual at Annwfn Land Sanctuary. Original words say, "Return to the land of your soul."

9. Cerridwen Fallingstar, "Persephone Rising," *Lesbian Tides Journal* (spring 1978).

10. Z. Budapest, "We All Come from the Goddess," unpublished chant.

11. Fallingstar, "Persephone Rising."

12. Tom F. Driver, "Ritual Theater and Sacrifice," *The Magic of Ritual: Our Needs for Rites That Transform Our Lives and Our Communities* (San Francisco: HarperSanFrancisco, 1991), 79–106.

13. Turner, *The Anthropology of Performance.*

14. Adapted from "Listen, Listen, Listen," by Paramahansa Yogananda, *Cosmic Chants* (Los Angeles: Self-Realization Fellowship, 1974). Original version reads,. "We shall never forsake you; we shall never forget you."

15. Traditional Wiccan benediction used to open the circle and complete a rite. Common usage, heard in many rituals throughout North America.

16. Dorothy Dinnerstein, *The Mermaid and the Minotaur* (New York: Harper & Row, 1976).

7. Feminism Meets Fertility Rites: May Day

1. Joanna Rogers Macy, *Despair and Personal Power in the Nuclear Age* (Philadelphia: New Society Publishers, 1983). This ritual form was originally developed by Chellis Glendinning in response to the Three Mile Island nuclear power accident.

2. Northup, *Ritualizing Women,* 39.

3. Naomi Wolf, *Promiscuities* (New York: Random House, 1997), 214–15.

4. Mary Collins, "Ritual Strategies in Feminist Ritual Events," paper given at the American Academy of Religion annual meeting, Ritual Studies section, Nov. 19, 1994, p. 7.

5. Ibid., 5.

6. Samuel Noah Kramer, *The Sacred Marriage Rite: Aspects of Faith, Myth, and Ritual in Ancient Sumer* (Bloomington: Indiana University Press, 1969). For discussion of the feminist implications of such practices, see Gerda Lerner, *The Creation of Patriarchy* (New York: Oxford University Press, 1986), 126–27, and Judith Ochshorn, *The Female Experience and the Nature of the Divine* (Bloomington: Indiana University Press, 1981).

7. Traditional English Maypole carol, which I first heard sung by the Berkeley Morris Dancers to sing the sun up on May Day morning. "Hull 'n tow" actually means "haul and tow," referring to the procedure of hauling the heavy Maypole up the hill for the festivities.

8. The Festival of First Fruits: Loaf Mass

1. Thorkild Jacobson, *Treasures of Darkness* (New Haven and London: Yale University Press 1976); Samuel Noah Kramer, *Sumerian Mythology* (New York: Harper & Brothers, 1961).
2. Rick Hamouris, "We Are a Circle," in *Welcome to Annwfn.*
3. Rick Hamouris, "Anthem to the Sun," in *Welcome to Annwfn.*
4. Rick Hamouris and Wendy Hunter Roberts, "Dance Away," *Evolution!* (1989).
5. De Beauvoir, *The Second Sex.* For more on solar goddesses, see Monaghan, *O Mother Sun!*
6. Genevieve Vaughan, *For-Giving* (Austin, Tex.: Plain View Press, 1997).
7. Wendy Hunter Roberts and Rick Hamouris, "Never You Fall," unpublished song, 1992.
8. Collins, "Principles of Feminist Liturgy," 11.
9. Ron L. Grimes, *Ritual Studies: Case Studies in Its Practices, Essays on Its Theory* (Columbia: University of South Carolina Press, 1990), 191–209.
10. Tom F. Driver, *The Magic of Ritual: Our Needs for Rites That Transform Our Lives and Our Communities* (San Francisco: HarperSanFrancisco, 1991), chaps. 6 and 7.

9. The Seven-Gated Passage: The Autumnal Equinox

1. Robin Morgan, "Revolucinations," in *Monster* (New York: Random House, 1972). The full stanza reads, "Men have forgotten how to love/women have forgotten how not to / We must risk unlearning/what has kept us alive," (54).
2. Arnold van Gannep, *Rites of Passage,* trans. Monika B. Vizedom and Gabrielle L. Caffee (Chicago: University of Chicago Press, 1960). Van Gannep coined the term "rites of passage" for rites that mark the transitional stages in human life, which he subdivided into rites of separation, transition rites, and rites of incorporation. He defined "a direct rite of passage by means of which a person leaves one world behind him and enters a new one" (19).
3. John E. Pfeiffer, The *Creative Explosion* (Ithaca, N.Y.: Cornell University Press, 1985).
4. See van Gannep, *Rites of Passage,* 20, 24, 57–61, for discussion of gates, portals, and thresholds in rites of passage.
5. Diane Wolkstein and Samuel Noah Kramer, "The Descent of Inanna," in *Inanna, Queen of Heaven and Earth* (New York: Harper & Row, 1983), 51–90. This ancient tale tells of the descent of the Sumerian Goddess through seven gates into the underworld. At each gate she had to leave behind some piece of finery, which distinguished her as Goddess, until she entered the final portals naked.
6. The mask I wore was the image of a predynastic Egyptian deity, Nekhbet, the great recycler of souls. The vulture was a symbol of transition in many ancient cultures. Ominous and frightening, but also sacred, she ushered animal life into the next realm, as seen in early Egyptian crypts and on the walls of Çatal Hüyük.

7. Chant heard in Halloween ritual at Annwfn Sanctuary, author unknown.

8. For a refreshing discussion of magic as the work of ritual transformation, see Tom F. Driver, *The Magic of Ritual,* chap. 9.

9. Van Gannep, in *Rites of Passage,* explains veiling the initiate for many rites of passage, saying the purpose is "to separate themselves from the profane and to live only in the sacred world, for seeing is itself a form of contact" (168).

10. Victor Turner, *The Ritual Process* (Baltimore: Penguin Books, 1969, 1974), 115.

11. The processes of future envisioning were adapted from Elise Boulding's work, in Warren L. Zeigler, *A Mindbook for Imaging/Inventing a World without Weapons,* 3d ed. (Denver: Futures-Invention Associates, 1983).

12. Driver, *The Magic of Ritual,* 137.

10. Ain't I a Woman: A Rite of Passage

1. Barbara Myerhoff, "Rites of Passage: Process and Paradox," in *Celebration,* ed. Victor Turner (Washington, D.C.: Smithsonian Institution Press, 1982), 109.

2. Ibid., 112.

3. Van Gannep, *Rites of Passage,* 85–86. In chapter 6, "Initiation Rites," van Gannep demonstrates at length that biological and social events do not generally converge in what are incorrectly referred to as puberty rites. He also illustrates the sexually oppressive nature of the rites, especially toward women and girls.

4. Ibid.

5. Naomi Wolf, *Promiscuities* (New York: Random House, 1997), 116–38.

6. Van Gannep, *Rites of Passage,* 21.

7. See Gerda Lerner, *History of Patriarchy* (New York: Oxford University Press, 1986), vol. 1:3–14, for discussion of the power to define and name and its relationship to women's emancipation.

8. Entire section adapted from Joanna Rogers Macy, "Learning to See Each Other," in *Despair and Personal Power in the Nuclear Age* (Philadelphia: New Society Publishers, 1983), 158–61.

9. Northup, *Ritualizing Women,* 44, 48.

10. Maya Angelou, *Phenomenal Woman* (New York: Random House), 1994.

11. Northup, *Ritualizing Women,* 42.

12. Collins, "Principles of Feminist Liturgy," 13.

BIBLIOGRAPHY

Adler, Margot. *Drawing Down the Moon*. Rev. ed. Boston: Beacon Press, 1986.

Angelou, Maya. *Phenomenal Woman*. New York: Random House, 1994.

Bell, Catherine. *Ritual Theory, Ritual Practice*. New York: Oxford University Press, 1992.

Budapest, Z. *Grandmother of Time*. San Francisco: HarperSanFrancisco, 1989.

——. *Holy Book of Women's Mysteries*. Wingbow Press, 1974.

——. *Summoning the Fates*. New York: Harmony, 1998.

Campanelli, Pauline. *Wheel of the Year*. St. Paul, Minn.: Llewelyn, 1989.

Caron, Charlotte. *To Make and Make Again: Feminist Ritual Theory*. New York: Crossroad Publishing, 1993.

Chodorow, Nancy. "Family Structure and Feminine Personality." In *The Homeric Hymn to Demeter*, edited by Helene P. Foley. Princeton, N.J.: Princeton University Press, 1994.

Christ, Carol. *Diving Deep and Surfacing: Women Writers on Spiritual Quest*. Boston: Beacon Press, 1980.

——. "Why Women Need the Goddess: Phenomenological, Psychological, and Political Reflections." In *The Politics of Women's Spirituality*, edited by Charlene Spretnak. New York: Anchor Books, 1982.

Collins, Mary. "Principles of Feminist Liturgy." In *Women at Worship*, edited by Marjorie Procter-Smith and Janet R. Walton. Louisville, Ky.: Westminster/John Knox, 1993.

Daly, Mary. *Beyond God the Father*. Boston: Beacon Press, 1973.

De Beauvoir, Simone. *The Second Sex*. Translated and edited by H. M. Parshley. New York: Knopf, 1952.

Diamond, Irene, and Gloria Orenstein, eds. *Reweaving the World: The Emergence of Ecofeminism*. San Francisco: Sierra Club Books, 1990.

Dinnerstein, Dorothy. *The Mermaid and the Minotaur*. New York: Harper & Row, 1976.

Driver, Tom F. *The Magic of Ritual: Our Needs for Rites That Transform Our Lives and Our Communities*. San Francisco: HarperSanFrancisco, 1991.

Eliade, Mircea. *A History of Religious Ideas from the Stone Age to the Eleusinian Mysteries*. Chicago: University of Chicago Press, 1978.

Fallingstar, Cerridwen. "Persephone Rising." *Lesbian Tides Journal*, spring 1978.

Faludi, Susan. *Backlash: The Undeclared War against American Women*. New York: Crown, 1991.

Foley, Helene P. "Gender Conflict and the Cosmological Tradition." In *The Homeric Hymn to Demeter*, edited by Helene P. Foley. Princeton, N.J.: Princeton University Press, 1994.

Foucault, Michel. *The History of Sexuality*. New York: Vintage Books, 1990.

Gadon, Elinor. *The Once and Future Goddess: A Symbol for Our Time*. San Francisco: Harper & Row, 1989.

Gimbutas, Marija. *The Civilization of the Goddess*. San Francisco: HarperSanFrancisco, 1991.

——. *The Goddesses and Gods of Old Europe, 6500 to 3500 B.C.E.* Berkeley: University of California Press, 1982.

——. *The Language of the Goddess*. San Francisco: Harper & Row, 1989.

Griffin, Susan. *Women and Nature: The Roaring inside Her*. New York: Harper & Row, 1978.

Grigolia, Mary. *Commitment to a Vision*. Self-published, 1989.

Grimes, Ronald L. *Ritual Criticism: Case Studies in Its Practices, Essays on Its Theory*. Columbia: University of South Carolina Press, 1990.

Hamouris, Rick and Deborah. *Welcome to Annwfn*. Redwood Valley, Calif.: Nemeton Publishing, 1986. Audiocassette.

Judith, Anodea. "Peruvian Pilgrimage." *The Green Egg* 93: 20–21.

Keller, Catherine. *From a Broken Web*. Boston: Beacon Press, 1986.

Klein, Ernest. *A Comprehensive Etymological Dictionary of the English Language*. Vol. 2. Amsterdam: Elsevier Publishing Company, 1967.

Kramer, Samuel Noah. *The Sacred Marriage Rite: Aspects of Faith, Myth, and Ritual in Ancient Sumer*. Bloomington: Indiana University Press, 1969.

Lerner, Gerda. *The Creation of Patriarchy*. New York: Oxford University Press, 1986.

McFague, Sallie. *The Body of God*. Minneapolis: Fortress Press, 1993.

Macy, Joanna Rogers. *Despair and Personal Power in the Nuclear Age*. Philadelphia: New Society Publishers, 1983.

Melaart, James. *Çatal Hüyük: A Neolithic Town in Anatolia*. London: Thames & Hudson, 1967.

Mitchell, Rosemary Catalano, and Gail Anderson Ricciuti. *Birthings and Blessings: Liberating Worship Services for the Inclusive Church*. New York: Crossroad Publishing, 1992.

Monaghan, Patricia. *O Mother Sun! A New View of the Cosmic Feminine*. San Francisco: HarperSanFrancisco: 1994.

Morgan, Robin. *Monster*. New York: Random House, 1972.

Murray, Margaret. *God of the Witches*. New York: Oxford University Press, 1931.

Myerhoff, Barbara. "Rites of Passage: Process and Paradox." In *Celebration*, edited by Victor Turner. Washington, D.C.: Smithsonian Institution Press, 1982.

Neu, Dianne L. "Liturgical Life of Women-Church: Defining Our Terms." In *Women-Church Sourcebook*, 2d ed., edited by Diann L. Neu and Mary E. Hunt. Silver Spring, Md.: Waterworks Press, 1993.

Northup, Lesley. *Ritualizing Women: Patterns of Spirituality*. Cleveland: The Pilgrim Press, 1997.

Ochshorn, Judith. *The Female Experience and the Nature of the Divine*. Bloomington: Indiana University Press, 1981.

Ortner, Sherry. "Is Female to Male as Nature Is to Culture?" In *Women and Values*, edited by Marilyn Pearsall. Belmont, Calif.: Wadsworth, 1986.

Paramahansa Yogananda. "Listen, Listen, Listen." *Cosmic Chants*. Los Angeles: Self-Realization Fellowship, 1974.

Pfeiffer, John E. *The Creative Explosion*. New York: Cornell University Press, 1985.

Phillips, John A. *Eve: The History of an Idea*. New York: Harper & Row, 1984.

Pintauro, Jose, and Alicia Bay Laurel. *The Earth Mass*. New York: Harper & Row, 1973.

Pomeroy, Sarah. *Goddesses, Whores, Wives, and Slaves: Women in Classical Antiquity*. New York: Schocken Books, 1975.

Procter-Smith, Marjorie. *In Her Own Rite: Constructing Feminist Liturgical Tradition*. Nashville: Abingdon, 1990.

————. *Praying with Our Eyes Open*. Nashville: Abingdon, 1995.

Procter-Smith, Marjorie, and Janet R. Walton, eds. *Women at Worship: Interpretations of North American Diversity.* Louisville, Ky.: Westminster/John Knox, 1993.

Ruether, Rosemary Radford. *Women Church: Theology and Practice.* San Francisco: Harper & Row, 1985.

Sender, Ramon. "Hymn to the Sun." In *Being of the Sun.* New York: Harper & Row, 1973.

Sjöö, Monica, and Barbara Mor. *The Great Cosmic Mother: Rediscovering the Religion of the Earth.* San Francisco: HarperSanFrancisco, 1991.

Springer, Heinrich (also known as Heinrich Institoris), and Jakob Kramer. *Malleus Maleficarum.* Brussels: Culture et Civilisation, originally published 1484, republished 1969.

Starhawk. *Dreaming the Dark: Magic, Sex, and Politics.* Boston: Beacon Press, 1982.

————. *Spiral Dance.* New York: Harper & Row, 1979.

Stein, Diane. *Casting the Circle.* Freedom, Calif.: Crossing Press, 1990.

Stone, Merlin. *When God Was a Woman.* New York: Dorset Press, 1976.

Turner, Kay. "Contemporary Feminist Rituals." In *The Politics of Women's Spirituality: Essays on the Rise of Spiritual Power within the Feminist Movement,* edited by Charlene Spretnak. New York: Doubleday, 1982.

Turner, Victor. *The Anthropology of Performance.* New York: PAJ Publications, 1986.

————. *Celebration.* Washington, D.C.: Smithsonian Institution Press, 1982.

————. *The Ritual Process.* Baltimore: Penguin Books, 1969.

Van Gannep, Arnold. *Rites of Passage.* Translated by Monika B. Vizedom and Gabrielle L. Caffee. Chicago: University of Chicago Press, 1960.

Vaughn, Genevieve. *For-Giving.* Austin, Tex.: Plain View Press, 1997.

Walker, Barbara. *Women's Rituals.* San Francisco: HarperSanFrancisco, 1990.

Warren, Karen J., ed. "Ecological Feminism." *Hypatia,* spring 1991.

Wittig, Monique. *Les Guerillères.* Translated by David Levay. New York: Avon Books, 1973.

Wolkstein, Diane, and Samuel Noah Kramer. *Inanna, Queen of Heaven and Earth.* New York: Harper & Row, 1983.

Zeigler, Warren L. *A Mindbook for Imaging/Inventing a World without Weapons.* 3d ed. Denver: Futures-Invention Associates, 1983.

INDEX